Curriculum Initiative:
An Agenda and Strategy for
Library Media Programs

Information Management, Policy, and Services

Charles R. McClure and Peter Hernon

Editors

Curriculum Initiative: An Agenda and Strategy for Library Media Programs
Michael B. Eisenberg and Robert E. Berkowitz

Microcomputer Software for Performing Statistical Analysis: A Handbook for Supporting Library Decision Making
Peter Hernon and John V. Richardson (Editors)

Resource Companion to Curriculum Initiative: An Agenda and Strategy for Library Media Programs
Michael B. Eisenberg and Robert E. Berkowitz

In preparation
Power, Politics, and Personality
June Engle

Managing Information for Competitive Positioning in Economic Development
Keith Harman

Public Access to Government Information, Revised Edition
Peter Hernon and Charles R. McClure

Assessing U.S. Government Information Policies: Issues and Options
Peter Hernon, Charles R. McClure and Harold C. Relyea

Microcomputer Graphics as a Library Resource
Bradford S. Miller

Curriculum Initiative:
An Agenda and Strategy for
Library Media Programs

Michael B. Eisenberg

Syracuse University
Syracuse, New York

Robert E. Berkowitz

Wayne Central School District
Ontario Center, New York

ABLEX PUBLISHING CORPORATION
Norwood, New Jersey

Fourth Printing 1993

Printed in the United States of America.

Library of Congress Cataloging-in-Publication Data

Eisenberg, Michael B.
    Curriculum initiative : an agenda and strategy for library media programs / by Michael B. Eisenberg, Robert E. Berkowitz.
      p. cm.—(Information management policy series)
    Includes index.
    ISBN 0-89391-486-X
    1. School libraries. 2. Media programs (Education) 3. Libraries and education. 4. Curriculum planning. I. Berkowitz, Robert E. II. Title. III. Series.
Z675.S3E35 1988
027.8—dc19   88-1598
                                                               CIP

Ablex Publishing Corporation
355 Chestnut St.
Norwood, NJ 07648

Contents

Acknowledgments   xiii

About the Authors   xv

Preface   xvii

Part I: Roles and Tools of the School Library Media Specialist   1

Chapter 1: Curriculum Concerns of the School Library Media
            Program   **3**

Chapter 2: Changing Roles of the School Library Media Specialist   **9**

Chapter 3: Basic Management Concepts and Tools   **15**

**Part II: The Six-Stage Strategy for Library Media Curriculum Program
Development and Management   27**

Chapter 4: Stage 1: Review Existing Situation   **29**
            Stage 2: Define Goals & Objectives   **29**

Chapter 5: Stage 3: Set Up Support Systems   **33**

Chapter 6: Stage 4: Conduct Feasibility Analysis   **43**

Chapter 7: Stage 5: Develop Plans   **51**
            Stage 6: Evaluate Plans and Processes   **51**

Part III: Curriculum: Information and Functions   69

Chapter 8: Curriculum Mapping: Collection, Organization and Evaluation
            of Curriculum Information   **71**

Chapter 9: Curriculum Support Services: Concerns of School Library
            Media Programs   **87**

Chapter 10: Library & Information Skills Curriculum: Scope and Sequence:
            The Big Six Skills   **99**

Chapter 11: Unit Plans and Lesson Plans   **121**

Chapter 12: A Look to the Future   **149**

Appendix A: Types of Sources/Systems to be Considered Under Location &
           Access Skills   **161**

Appendix B: Time Management Study   **163**

Bibliography   **167**

Author Index   **171**

Subject Index   **173**

List of Figures

Figure 3.1   Educational Contexts   **16**

Figure 3.2   Systems Approach   **17**

Figure 3.3   Problem-Solving Model from *The Universal Traveler*   **21**

Figure 3.4   Problem-Solving Feedback Perspective from *The Universal Traveler*   **23**

Figure II   Strategy Flow   **28**

Figure 5.1   An Example of an Organization Structure for a School   **36**

Figure 6.1   Feasibility   **44**

Figure 6.2   Time Demand v. Availability   **48**

Figure 7.1   Structure for Five-Year Plan   **52**

Figure 7.2   Alternate Structure for a Five-Year Plan   **53**

Figure 7.3a   Elementary School Schedule of Subject Area Units   **55**

Figure 7.3b   Secondary School Schedule of Selected Subject Area Units   **56**

Figure 7.4a   Elementary School Skills by Unit Matrix   **58**

Figure 7.4b   Secondary School Skills by Unit Matrix   **59**

Figure 7.5a   Elementary School Support Services by Unit Matrix   **61**

Figure 7.5b   Secondary School Curriculum Support Services by Unit Matrix   **62**

Figure 7.6   Elementary School Year Schedule: includes Big Six Skills, curriculum support services, and comments   **63**

Figure 8.1   Elements/Fields of Interest for Curriculum Maps   **74**

Figure 8.2   Curriculum Mapping Worksheet   **75**

Figure 8.3   Curriculum Map Database Definition Using dBase II or III (on IBM)   **77**

Figure 8.4   Curriculum Map Database Definition Using Appleworks (on Apple II)   **78**

Figure 8.5   Curriculum Map Database Definition Using Reflex (on Apple Macintosh)   **78**

Figure 8.6   Elementary Curriculum Map (full information sorted by grade/calendar quarter)   **79**

Figure 8.7   Elementary Curriculum Map (information sorted by subject, resources = multiple, evaluation not test)   **80**

Figure 8.8   Elementary Curriculum Map: K–3 (focus on variables of instruction)   **81**

Figure 8.9   Secondary Curriculum Map (full information sorted by grade/calendar quarter)   **82**

Figure 8.10   Secondary Curriculum Map: Grades 10–12 (major units, 10 or more periods, sorted by periods and grades)   **82**

Figure 9.1   Resources Provision Services Checklist   **90**

Figure 9.2   Reading Guidance Services Checklist   **92**

Figure 9.3   Information Services Checklist   **93**

Figure 9.4   Curriculum Consultation Services Checklist   **95**

Figure 9.5   Curriculum Development Services Checklist   **97**

Figure 10.1   Overview of the Big Six Skills   **101**

Figure 10.2   Bloom's Cognitive Levels and Associated Information Oriented Actions   **102**

Figure 10.3   Questions Linked to Bloom's Cognitive Levels   **103**

Figure 10.4   The Active Thinking Vocabulary   **104**

Figure 10.5   The Big Six Skills: A Library & Information Skills Curriculum   **108**

Figure 11.1   Unit Plan Format   **125**

Figure 11.2   Lesson Plan Format   **128**

Figure 12.1   Library Media Program/Curriculum Relationship: Phase 1   **155**

Figure 12.2   Library Media Program/Curriculum Relationship: Phase 2   **156**

Figure 12.3   Library Media Program/Curriculum Relationship: Phase 3   **156**

Figure 12.4   Library Media Program/Curriculum Relationship: Phase 4   **157**

Figure 12.5   Library Media Program/Curriculum Relationship: Phase 5   **157**

Figure B.1   Time Management Study   **165**

To Carol, Brian, and Laura, for your patience, understanding, and support;

To Joyce, Adam, and Marette, who heard, "Papa's gotta work on the book," all too often—you teach me about unconditional love.

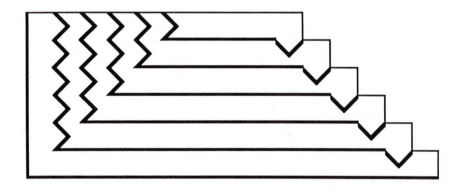

Acknowledgments

Often it is difficult to discover how and by whom ideas are nurtured, especially in a profession that is constantly evolving. Just as continuous dialogue shaped our present partnership, our separate pasts were influenced by many people. The following persons have, to one degree or another, knowingly or unknowingly, contributed to the development of our ideas. We jointly acknowledge them because of their influence on us as individuals and therefore as partners. Evelyn Daniel, a very special friend, as well as Richard Halsey and James Liesener are academic mentors who became colleagues and continue to affect our outlook. Additionally, Rao Lindsay is a lingering influence as he goads us into searching for the purpose behind the practice. Elliot and Eleanor Goldstein generously share their ideas, resources, and commitment. John Cooper encourages educators to seek out and seize opportunities for continued professional growth. Ron Miller provides thoughtful consideration and a measured response to professional concerns. These administrators as well as Paul Preuss and Charlie Slick understand the importance of the library media specialist to today's schools. Our library media specialist colleagues throughout New York State, especially our associates in NYLA and SLMS, provided an early forum for our ideas. We owe a special thanks to past and present students in our "curriculum concerns" and "library media management" classes, particularly Christine Lauster, Judith Gordon, Gail Bieszad, and Sharon Voninski, who contributed substantively to this book. Those colleagues and friends who support the goals of the library media program at Wayne Central and Fayetteville-Manlius, as well as the other school districts where we've worked as professionals or consultants, all deserve recognition. The names are many, but particularly Joan and Chuck Imhoff and Betty Taber, who spent extra time to share in the enthusiasm of the discovery, the F-M Humanities Group whose zest for creativity and innovation was contagious, and Gaby Hendley who set the finest of examples. To Tim Jackson, Carol Notowitz, Linda Perla, Jeane Rinker, Carolyn Trombly, Helaine Zinaman, Janet Sassaman, Bob and Harriet Spilsbury, Al and Vinnie Casatelli, Sara Kelly Brenizer, Tim and Linda McNerney, John and Martha Obrycki, and those unnamed, who listened to ideas and dreams, we are grateful. Appreciation is also expressed to Linda Schamber for her keen editing eye. Finally, our thanks to Chuck McClure who provided us with this opportunity, and whose timely encouragement redefined the word "finished."

People who help nuture ideas give gifts to us all. These are such people.

Mike Eisenberg & Bob Berkowitz
September 1987

About the Authors

Michael B. Eisenberg (PhD Syracuse University, MLS State University of New York at Albany) is an Assistant Professor at the School of Information Studies, Syracuse University. His research and teaching interests include management and curriculum concerns of school media programs, the use of information systems by end users, and the measurement and evaluation of information systems. In addition to teaching and research, Mike's responsibilities at Syracuse include coordination of the School Library Media Program and the Assistant Director position at the ERIC Clearinghouse on Information Resources. Mike's publications include: "Curriculum Mapping and Implementation of an Elementary School Library Media Skills Curriculum, *School Library Media Quarterly: The Direct Use of Information Systems by Untrained End-Users,* ERIC, 1982; and "Managing the Library and Information Skills Program," *School Library Media Activities Monthly* (March 1986). His 1986 doctoral thesis, *Magnitude Estimation and the Measurement of Relevance,* won national awards from both the American Society for Information Science and the Association for Library and Information Science Education. Mike is a frequent speaker at conferences and presents a number of workshops and training sessions each year. He has worked as a teacher, school library media specialist, program administrator, and consultant.

Robert E. Berkowitz, School Library Media Specialist, currently with the Wayne Central School District, Ontario Center, New York, has successfully managed school libraries grades Head Start–12 in both rural and urban settings. He has been an educational professional since 1971. Bob received his Master of Arts in Education from The George Washington University, Washington, D.C., and his Master of Library Science from the State University of New York at Albany. Recently, he completed his School Administrator's Certification requirements at North Adams (Massachusetts) State College. He is co-founder of SCAN: School Library Career Awareness Network in New York State. Bob is a strong believer in goals-oriented management, the library media specialist as a key partner in curriculum development, the library media specialist as an active partner in the excellence in education—effective schools movement, and the integration of critical thinking skills into library & information skills instruction. Putting these ideas into practice, Bob acted as Library Media Specialist consultant to a research skills-based English curriculum project that won National Council of

Teachers of English recognition as a Center of Excellence in English and the Language Arts. He is often requested to share his ideas at conferences and seminars across New York State. Bob is an Adjunct Lecturer at Syracuse University's School of Information Studies. He is the author of "Thinking is Critical: Moving Students Beyond Location," *School Library Media Activities Monthly* (May 1987), and "Marketing the School Library Media Center: a Process for Success," *The Book Report* (May/June 1987). Bob has a strong commitment to library media specialists shaping their own professional future.

Preface

This book is intended to provide practicing school library media specialists and students in professional degree-granting programs with both a conceptual framework and practical approaches to the curriculum-related responsibilities of the school library media program. These responsibilities involve library & information skills instruction and curriculum support services.

Curriculum provides the framework for continuity at all levels of education. It is the center of the educational process, encompassing the objectives of instruction and the scope and sequence of content. Curriculum relates to the specifics of what is taught, in what order, by what methods, with what materials and resources, and how it is evaluated. The administration of curriculum and its components, (course content, time frame and sequence, teaching methodologies, instructional materials, evaluation methods) is a difficult, yet attainable, task.

The major roles of the school library media professional are concerned with curriculum. From early on, the school library (and later the school library media center) has been responsible for providing support materials to students and teachers. As we move forward into the information age, access to a broad range of materials and sources has become even more important. Library media specialists are becoming increasingly involved in all phases of curriculum: development, support, consultation, and implementation.

In this book, we present and argue for a new definition of the curriculum support services role for the library media program. We view curriculum support services as five interrelated areas: (1) curriculum resources provision, (2) reading guidance, (3) information service, (4) curriculum consultation, and (5) curriculum development. This is an active perspective that contributes to extending the influence of the library media program into every major aspect of the educational program.

Furthermore, the library media program has a curriculum of its own to implement. Beyond the modest, traditional concerns of locating and accessing sources, today's library media programs need to provide structured and planned opportunities for students to develop a full range of library & information skills. In order to live in an information-based society, students need to be able to solve information problems. To this end, we offer the *Big Six Skills* curriculum based on the information problem-solving process of task definition, information-seeking strategies, location and access, information use, synthesis, and evaluation.

Library & information skills are most effectively learned when integrated with the needs and activities of the classroom. This makes sense from both practical and conceptual perspectives. The goals of this book are to identify library & information skills curriculum objectives, and to provide a mechanism for integrating library & information skills instruction within the framework of subject area curricula.

These two major curriculum-related functions—curriculum support services and library & information skills instruction—must be systematically approached and implemented by library media programs. To assist in this effort, we offer the *Six-Stage Strategy* for library media curriculum program development and management. This is a systematic planning strategy to develop the curriculum-related functions of the library media program within the context of a school's overall curriculum program.

In order to implement a meaningful program of curriculum support services and integrated library & information skills instruction, the library media specialist must know overall curriculum goals and objectives of the school, actual classroom curriculum activities, and have a good working relationship with teachers and administrators. The *Six-Stage Strategy* is a tested, successful process for use by library media specialists in creating effective curriculum programs.

The role and relationship of library media professionals to curriculum is changing. A movement toward an integral role both in curriculum development and delivery and in teaching fundamental skills is gaining momentum. The need to maintain this momentum involves strengthening collaboration with teachers and administrators. Library media professionals need to meet this challenge with a positive and systematic response. In doing so, the library media center will achieve status as an educational setting for content learning as well as for library & information skills learning. The pervading intent of this book is to present a well-constructed, unified model for approaching this changing role. This model is not a prescription; we do not anticipate that library media specialists will undertake each step exactly as presented. Rather, we present a description of tested, effective techniques that can be adapted to local situations and aid library media specialists in dealing with the difficult tasks associated with curriculum.

The book is organized in three sequential parts:

Part I provides the groundwork by describing the roles and tools of the library media program. Included is an overview of curriculum concerns, a look at how the roles of the library media specialist have changed over time, and an introduction to management concepts and tools that form the basis for tasks and approaches suggested later.

Part II outlines in detail the Six-Stage Strategy for developing and managing curriculum-related functions of the library media program. The intention here is to provide a systematic strategy for approaching curriculum program concerns. Each step and tool in the strategy is adaptable to individual situations, and it is not necessary to adopt every activity and task suggested. However, it is important to be systematic and deliberate in approaching curriculum concerns.

Part III provides additional detail and depth on (1) collection and organization of curriculum information, (2) curriculum support services, and (3) a library & information skills curriculum: the Big Six Skills, and (4) unit and lesson planning. The curriculum concerns of the library media program center on these areas. The book concludes with a look to the future.

Throughout the writing, there has been a healthy tension between the authors. While immediately agreeing with the overall purpose and objectives of this book, each author has his own unique style and perspective. Early on, the authors agreed to bring their separate ideas together. Each challenged the other to explain and justify his ideas within the context of the curriculum role as defined. From this emerged the conceptualization of the curriculum support services role, the Big Six Skills curriculum, and the the Six-Stage Strategy.

In this book you will be introduced to concepts, ideas, problems, and solutions in a logical sequence. To us, planning and action are synonymous. We hope the material presented will excite you and challenge you to take action.

PART I

ROLES AND TOOLS OF THE SCHOOL LIBRARY MEDIA SPECIALIST

Part I introduces the curriculum concerns and responsibilities of the school library media program. Two central areas of concern emerge: (1) curriculum support services and (2) the library & information skills curriculum.

Chapter 1 outlines the factors that comprise these concerns and describes the relationship between the library media program and the overall educational program. Chapter 2 traces the evolution of the role of the library media specialist from passive, narrow origins to active, expanded responsibilities. Chapter 3 discusses management tools and concepts that can assist the library media specialist in meeting curriculum needs. These tools and concepts are the basis for the Six-Stage Strategy and other recommended planning mechanisms.

CHAPTER 1

Curriculum Concerns of the School Library Media Program

This chapter introduces the major curriculum concerns of the library media program. These concerns are based on school goals, objectives, and ultimately the actual curriculum as carried out in classrooms. Concerns also involve curriculum support services, the library & information skills curriculum, and the relationship of the library media program to classroom content. Problem areas within these concerns are identified.

• • •

Curriculum is the conceptual heart of the educational process. Curriculum translates educational goals into learning experiences, and describes the specific interactions of students, teachers and subject matter. For curriculum to succeed in an information–rich world, availability of, access to, and use of a wide range of resources are crucial. To this end, the classroom needs to incorporate outside information with the traditional textbook approach. This need for a broad-based approach to instructional resources makes the library media center the ultimate classroom. A broad-based, information–oriented approach to education puts students in a position to attain subject area curriculum goals as well as library media curriculum goals. The skills associated with acquiring and using information therefore become integrated with course content and basic for all students.

As curriculum is central to the educational process, so too, is the library media program central to curriculum. The library media specialist, trained as an information professional, can play a key role. The skills and abilities that library media specialists bring to the educational arena include selection and evaluation, organization, provision of services and resources, instruction, and consultation with teachers and students. With these competencies, the library media specialist has the capacity to make the library media program the foundation for, an integral part of, and an extension to the total school curriculum.

DISTRICT AND SCHOOL GOALS AND OBJECTIVES

One of the common characteristics of effective schools is a statement of purpose encompassing the goals and objectives of the school. This *mission statement* acts as the basis for curriculum decisions and provides overriding direction for all activities. In order to participate successfully in any aspect of curriculum, the library media specialist must be aware of and clearly understand the school's stated purpose.

However, a written statement of goals and objectives is not always readily available. Furthermore, even if such a document exists, it may not accurately reflect the current orientation of the school. Therefore, the library media specialist must be able to discern hidden agendas and be able to recognize and articulate general, pervading orientations.

CURRICULUM CONCERNS

In some instances the official written curriculum of a school is in fact not the same as the curriculum taught. Often curriculum is adapted, rather than adopted, to meet particular student/teacher/administrator considerations. If the curriculum functions of support, consultation, and development are to be carried out efficiently and effectively by library media professionals, it is essential that information about the school's curriculum be systematically collected and organized. Curriculum mapping is a proven, effective technique for compiling, storing, and retrieving information about real aspects of curriculum (sequence, level, time frame, scope, methods, evaluation, etc.). With the kind of information provided by curriculum mapping, the library media specialist is in an informed position and able to plan for and deliver necessary support services and integrated library & information skills instruction.

Traditionally (and minimally), the library media program has offered support to curriculum through the provision of materials. The school library media specialist, essentially outside the curriculum development process, has generally acted only in a resource or support capacity. There is, however, potential for a much more active role for the library media specialist in curriculum support. While education is becoming increasingly information-dependent, few teachers or administrators are knowledgeable, experienced, or comfortable about matters pertaining to information resources, systems, and the use of information in curriculum and instruction.

Library media specialists know how to access, use, and evaluate information. They know the appropriate strategies for seeking relevant information and how to use that information for meeting stated objectives (in assignments, for example). Therefore, the library media specialist can assume a role as consultant on the use of information in curriculum. This places the library media specialist in a position central to the development and implementation of the total school curriculum.

Too often in the past, school library media specialists have acted as minor partners in developing instructional materials and curriculum consultants only after the fact. However, in an educational climate calling for excellence and based on the use of information and developing critical thinking skills, library media specialists have both the opportunity and the responsibility to make a positive impact on the quality of learning, school-wide. Therefore, within the phrase *curriculum support services*, this book assumes an expanded role beyond resources support involving direct information service, reading guidance, curriculum consultation, and curriculum development.

In addition to providing a full range of curriculum support services, the library media program has its own curriculum agenda: the *library & information skills* curriculum. This use of the phrase "library & information skills" rather than "library skills" or "library media skills" is intentional. The learning outcomes and objectives relating to information extend beyond mere location and access to resources. It is essential that educated human beings understand and use a systematic process for information problem-solving. In this book, this information problem-solving process is presented as the *Big Six Skills* comprised of (1) task definition, (2) information-seeking strategy, (3) location and access, (4) use of information, (5) synthesis, and (6) evaluation. Seeing that students acquire these skills is a vital concern of the library media program.

Of course, the library & information skills curriculum must be founded on the overriding goals of the total school program. Current educational concerns with critical thinking skills, lifetime learning, and the basics of literacy, writing, and computation directly link school goals to the library media program.

In practical terms, the realization of the goals and objectives of a school is the curriculum as carried out in classrooms. Therefore, the dual curriculum-related aspects of the library media program (i.e., curriculum support services and library & information skills instruction) must be integrally involved with classroom content. The points of intersection between classroom content and library curriculum are the the the optimal teaching opportunities for library & information skills instruction.

Beyond the practical value of teaching library & information skills in a classroom curriculum context, it also makes educational sense to align these skills with classroom content. If done successfully, a library & information skills curriculum becomes integral to the overall effort of teaching students how to think independently. At the very highest level, there is more than an integrated curriculum; the overall school curriculum is actually *information-based* and the library media center becomes as common a setting for content learning as the classroom.

A STRATEGY FOR IMPLEMENTING EFFECTIVE CURRICULUM SUPPORT SERVICES AND LIBRARY & INFORMATION SKILLS INSTRUCTION

Curriculum concerns vary with the level of involvement of the library media program within the educational arena, but essentially involve:

- an information problem (knowing the curriculum);
- a service problem (meeting the needs of the curriculum);
- a design problem (identifying essential library & information skills);
- a communication problem (publicizing the curriculum-related roles); and
- a management problem (planning for the curriculum-related program).

This book addresses these problems through a model called the *Six-Stage Strategy*. The Six-Stage Strategy is not some academic exercise. It is based on problem-solving methods and approaches tested and revised in real library media settings. Furthermore, it is not a dogmatic, prescriptive approach. It is fully recognized that some aspects may be more applicable to particular situations than others; that some aspects will be expanded locally, others ignored. Regardless of whether one is involved with a new situation, concerned with meeting new demands, or just simply interested in re-examining the current state of affairs, the Six Stage Strategy offers effective tools and techniques for review and planning.

POSITIONING THE LIBRARY MEDIA PROGRAM FOR CURRICULUM ACTION

Although some library media specialists will react with immediate enthusiasm to the ideas and approaches presented in this book, others may be more cautious. This book is intended for the reserved as well as the eager. In particular, there is a concern with assisting those persons thinking, "how do I begin to develop curriculum-oriented functions when I can't even get the teachers and administrators to cooperate?"

It is certainly true that some library media specialists are faced with difficult situations. There are school systems in which library media professionals are forced to cover more than one building. Others have a full-day schedule of classes and little or no support staff. And still others are faced with schools that have a long history of non-involvement with the library media center.

Recognizing that serious problems do exist, library media specialists must still strive to provide meaningful programs. This is mandated by the vital instructional opportunities and services that quality library media programs are able to offer and by the importance of information skills and information resources in modern education. In every setting, ways must be found to redirect and improve the library media program and the relationship of the program to subject area curriculum. Initially, objectives may need to be limited, and progress toward meeting objectives may be slow. But movement and change are still possible.

The agenda and strategy presented in this book are relevant to all library media contexts. For those programs already involved in significant curriculum-related functions, this book offers new perspectives and a range of tools for moving even further. But perhaps even more importantly, for those library media specialists in more difficult situations, this book offers the direction and systematic means necessary to begin.

Requirements for a successful curriculum initiative can be summarized in four simple yet powerful words:

- attitude;
- approach;
- agenda; and
- action.

First and foremost, a positive, energetic attitude can go a long way to effecting change. Conversely, a defeatist attitude all but assures failure. A positive attitude does not mean adopting an unrealistic, Pollyanna demeanor. It means that when new situations or demands arise, they are immediately viewed not as overbearing problems, but as challenges. Regardless of previous patterns or experiences, opportunities for improvement do exist. A positive attitude is infectious—picked up by teachers, administrators, and students. Without an open, positive attitude, chances of success are minimal.

Of course, a positive attitude by itself is not enough. One of the additional requirements for success is a systematic, organized approach to planning, development, and implementation. Library media specialists are generally viewed as persons who approach issues and problems in highly-organized, professional ways. In addition, the library media specialist should be seen as someone who knows what needs to be accomplished and who moves to get it done. This calls for a certain confident and assertive style; not overly demanding, but highly committed and motivated.

An agenda refers to having an understanding and vision of what it is you hope to accomplish. If all things were possible, if there were no restrictions due to staff, facilities, resources, or funds, what would you be looking to do? Then, in light of the real situation, what do you realistically expect to be able to attain? This book offers a fully-developed agenda focusing on meeting the curriculum needs of students, teachers, and administrators. The agenda outlines (1) a full range of curriculum support services and (2) a direct, problem-solving approach to library & information skills instruction. These two information-based functions are appropriate and vital to all educational settings. Library media specialists must formulate agendas that meet the demands and reality of their own schools. These are customized, individualized plans that recognize limitations but also strive to move schools beyond the status quo.

Ultimately, there must be action. Library media specialists cannot sit around and wait for the curriculum to come to them. Agendas must be shared and promoted with teachers and administrators. Library media professionals must take the initiative, make the first move, and if necessary, make the second and third move as well. Every day, administrators and teachers face their own problems and demands. Many have fallen into habits and patterns that do not regularly include the library media program. Therefore, library media specialists must reach out and demonstrate what is possible and how library media services can make an impact on specific classes as well as on the overall school program.

Long-standing patterns are not completely changed overnight, but it is possible to set realistic goals, and make slow and steady progress to attain them. For example, if there is little cooperation from teachers, start with the one or two teachers who appear most receptive. Or if schedule demands are heavy, choose one curriculum-related service to emphasize and develop.

There are numerous ideas, skills, systems, and processes described and promoted in this text. At first glance, it might seem easier to say: I can't possibly do these given the current state of my program, resources, and support by administrators and teachers. It is precisely those library media specialists in difficult situations who can least afford to ignore the agenda and strategy suggested in this book. View the material with caution if you wish, but also view it as an opportunity.

Before turning to an explanation of the strategy and its implementation, it is important to put a historical perspective on the role of the library media specialist in relation to curriculum. That is, how has the role evolved over time, what is involved, and what can it become?

CHAPTER 2

Changing Roles of the School Library Media Specialist

It has been said that there are no constants, only constant change. This maxim is certainly true for the role of the school library media specialist. Today, there is an increasing reliance on technology in education. Likewise, the information explosion is forcing a move away from single-source, textbook-based instruction to a more information-based education. Both these developments point to a central leadership role for an information and systems professional—namely the school library media specialist. This role represents an expansion of traditional roles as well as an extension into new areas. Periodically during the past three and a half decades, consistent patterns have been observed in the changing roles for the school library media professional. This chapter examines:

- the traditional roles of the school library media specialist;
- the evolution of traditional roles;
- the development in new areas of competency and responsibility; and
- expectations for the future.

LITERATURE ON THE ROLES OF THE MEDIA SPECIALIST

The literature in the school library media area is rich in discussions, papers, and articles delving into the functions and responsibilities of school library media specialists. Recent efforts include Ely (1982), Hortin (1985), Craver (1986), and Mancall, Aaron and Walker (1986). Definitions and descriptions are abundant in texts on school library media programs (e.g., Prostano and Prostano, 1982; Davies, 1979; Chisholm and Ely, 1976; Shapiro, 1975) or in the national standards (American Association of School Librarians, 1960, 1969, 1975).

Craver (1986) provides an excellent survey of the changing instructional role of the school media specialist by reviewing historical information provided in journal articles, national standards, research studies, and monographs. Also worth special attention is the Fall 1986 issue of *School Library Media Quarterly* devoted to the topic of the role of library media program development in "educating students to think." The Mancall, Aaron, and Walker (1986) position paper is the cornerstone of the issue.

This chapter will not cover the same ground as these fine resources. The intent here is to provide a composite view of the changing role of the media specialist and highlight major themes and trends.

TRADITIONAL ROLES

From early on, the role of the school "librarian" has been seen as encompassing three major areas:

1. collection management;
2. reading guidance and the promotion of literature; and
3. reference and information service.

The foundation of the role of the modern school media specialist is also based in the traditional responsibilities of collection development and management. These responsibilities include collection building, organization, access and delivery, maintenance, and evaluation. The function of promoting reading and the appreciation of literature is a natural complement to the collection management role. Similarly, assisting students with locating and using information sources is fundamental to traditional librarianship and fits nicely with collection and literature responsibilities.

PATTERNS AND TRENDS

In an examination of change in these fundamental roles, a number of discernible patterns emerge. First, in all three of these areas, a steady increase in the level of involvement and expansion of functions has occurred. Responsibilities do not seem to diminish in some areas while others increase; instead, there is a continual widening of scope in collections, promotion of literature, and reference services.

In some cases the change is more than an extension of traditional roles. For example, formal library & information skills instruction goes well beyond the original function of reference and information service and can stand alone as a major functional area. This teaching role of the library media specialist is the most dramatic and far-reaching extension of a traditional function.

A second recognizable pattern is the change from passive to active in the execution of these functions. In the development process, the passive approach means having materials and services available for use by students and faculty, but leaving initiation of contact up to the patron. At some point, in each responsibility area, this passive attitude is replaced by an active, more assertive stance. There is an attempt to reach out to users, promote services and collections, and become more directly involved in the research process and the use of information. Craver (1986) documents the general movement from passive "keeper of materials" to an active participant in the educational process. As with the pattern of expanding functions, the role of the library media specialist as teacher of information skills represents a vivid example of the movement from passive to active.

The third noticeable trend is a disparity in perceptions of the role of the library media specialist. Ely (1982) notes the gap between internal perceptions within the profession and the perceptions of others, particularly administrators and teachers. He points to the Conant study (1980) finding that, "There is no commonly understood or accepted concept among educators as to what a media center is or should be, and therefore no firmly established expectations of media center personnel." Media specialists have long decried the lack of understanding and proper use of library media services by teachers and administrators.

A similar gap exists between the viewpoints expressed in the professional literature and actual practice. Hortin (1985) reported that, while in theory the duties of today's school media specialist place greater emphasis on involvement in curriculum development, instructional design, and production, few professionals actually do much in the way of instructional development. Craver (1986) notes that although clear and substantive progress in the development of the instructional role of the media specialist is reflected in the literature and standards, research studies point to a delay in the implementation of these developments.

BEYOND TRADITIONAL ROLES

The trends noted above, particularly the expansion of the scope of responsibilities and the evolution from passive to active approach, can be observed in each of the three major areas. For example, the collection role now encompasses the promotion of collection use beyond the walls of the library media center. This expanded role includes consultation with teachers on resources for instruction and a range of awareness and promotion activities including booktalks, bibliographies and resource lists, and presentations to classes. The collections management function has also grown to include a wide range of materials, print and nonprint, in a unified media center concept.

The movement from a "collection caretaker" perspective to a "provider of appropriate materials" has influenced the reading guidance function as well. Beyond offering a quality collection of fiction and nonfiction, the library media specialist is now involved in the aggressive promotion of reading, literature, and literacy. This expanded role often involves library media specialists directly in teaching situations. Curriculum guides (e.g., New York State Elementary Library Media Skills Curriculum, 1980) discuss close cooperation and coordination with the language arts program to provide an integrated approach. In many cases, the library media specialist is engaged in a range of coordinated activities (e.g., booktalks, "Parents as Reading Partners") which seek to involve teachers and parents in literature and reading promotion. In other situations, literature and reading guidance activities are still carried out in isolation.

The trends of expansion of scope and more active involvement are easily seen in the reference and information service areas as well. Approach and attitude have moved well beyond simply providing reference materials and responding to questions when asked. Library media specialists seek to anticipate students' needs and situations where information service will be required. Concerns have grown beyond "access to materials" to encompass information use, manipulation, and evaluation within the overall research process.

As noted previously, this expansion of roles is most clearly seen in the development of library skills instruction programs. Today, the direct teaching of library & information skills to students through formal instruction is a central component of active reference and information services. In this capacity, the library media specialist is a teacher with an established curricular agenda, teaching objectives, and planned lessons.

It has been widely argued that an effective skills program is best accomplished in conjunction with classroom instruction (see Walker and Montgomery, 1983). Library & information skills are best taught when integrated and combined with subject objectives and content. Unfortunately, in too many situations the library skills program has been implemented as an isolated, separate subject. Therefore, a major theme in current literature and professional meetings is the movement from a non-aligned approach and tightly scheduled classes to a unified approach coordinated with classroom instruction.

The augmentation of the reference role to include direct teaching has visibly affected how media specialists spend their time. Direct instructional responsibilities require more training and background in teaching, methodology, and curriculum. Certification requirements, library school programs, and the literature all reflect these additional skills.

In addition to the expansion of teaching library & information skills, both the reference and collections management have expanded into a more global curriculum *consultant* role. Beyond simply providing materials, library media specialists are increasingly involved with how materials are used, by whom, and for what purpose. In addition to knowledge of materials, library media specialists must be aware of curriculum, teaching methods, instructional design considerations, and evaluation. Media specialists' competencies related to instructional design both parallel and overlap the curriculum roles. Ely (Gerlach and Ely, 1980; Chisholm and Ely, 1976, 1979) has written extensively on the instructional design role and the need for media professionals to be involved with teaching-learning strategies, instructional media, and recommendations about the media most appropriate for attaining stated objectives. This requires familiarity and competence with a wide range of learning technologies.

To date, the activities associated with curriculum and instructional media have not been fully realized. This exemplifies the gap between literature and practice noted above. Yes, there are library media specialists acting in important curriculum and instructional design capacities; however, overall, practice lags behind theory. In examining the major trends of each decade, Craver (1986) points out a clear, substantive expansion in the instructional role of the media specialist from "study hall monitor to curriculum designer." While this is true to some degree, there is still much more to be done.

Responsibilities associated with computer technology provide a final example of the trends noted above. Here again, trends include: a building on traditional functions, a movement from passive to active, and discernible gaps between internal and external perceptions. At the most fundamental level, the library media specialist is responsible for materials provision, i.e., providing users with access to machines and software. All the traditional competencies of selection and evaluation, collection management and promotion come into play. Second, there is the promotion of literacy—in this case, technological or computer literacy. Third, the availability of reference sources and information via computers (online information utilities, microcomputer-based databases, compact discs, etc.) require library media specialists to use these materials and to instruct students in their use.

The level of computer-related involvement by library media specialists varies considerably across programs. Some specialists have moved extensively into online search services; others have assumed full computer coordination responsibilities. Still others are fighting for initial access to a microcomputer. Based on the trends noted above, it seems reasonable to expect steady progress and involvement in the computer area. (For more on media specialists and computers see Cook and Truett, 1984; Woolls and Loertscher, 1986; Costa and Costa, 2nd edition, 1986).

ROLES REDEFINED

The centrality and importance of modern school library media specialists in education seem clear. Contributing factors are: (1) the increasing use of technology in education (computers, video, telecommunications); (2) the information explosion and the move to more information-based education, (3) the emphasis on preparation for lifetime learning reflected in national reports on education (e.g. *A Nation at Risk*, 1983), and (4) the acceptance by many library media specialists of new responsibilities and roles, including the use of new technologies when appropriate.

A definable role, based on traditional functions but responsive to a changing world, is emerging. This role includes:

1. collection management based on a unified media concept;
2. promotion of literacy, and guidance in the use of media;
3. teaching information skills for an information society, through integration with classroom curriculum;

4. acting as a catalyst or agent of change in schools through awareness of cutting-edge technology and consultation on curriculum and instructional design; and
5. assuming information management responsibilities beyond the walls of the centralized library media facility.

This role may be best summarized as a *mediation function* as described by Liesener (1984): the library media professional is the intermediary between the increasingly complex and rapidly expanding world of information and the client. Similarly, the Council on Library and Network Development of the Wisconsin Department of Public Instruction has taken the position that "the search for solutions to educational problems must include library media specialists as information specialists in this information era." (Diehl et al., 1984)

Considerable variety and flexibility exist within this vision. Ely (1982) notes that today there is no single composite model of a school library media specialist. Each media specialist creates his or her own role within a broad range of possibilities. While this may be frustrating to some degree, it is also the natural response to a changing environment. The trends of expansion, further development, and passive-to-active involvement will naturally continue. The primary challenge is to narrow the gaps between theory and practice, and between internal and external perceptions and expectations. Library media specialists are increasingly assuming the role described above. The users of library media service—students, teachers, administrators, and parents—must come to value, expect, and if necessary, demand high-quality library media programs.

• • •

This book is an effort to meet this challenge by providing both a conceptual and practical framework for implementation of a full range of curriculum support services and an integrated, information problem-solving approach to library & information skills instruction.

Before moving to the specifics of the Six-Stage Strategy, the book discusses general management concepts and tools in chapter 3.

CHAPTER 3

Basic Management Concepts and Tools

Certain management approaches can greatly aid the library media specialist in designing, planning, and providing for effective curriculum-related activities. The objectives of this chapter are to:

- view the school library media program within a systems framework;
- suggest a systematic approach to planning and problem-solving;
- identify and set up necessary support systems;
- offer the Six-Stage Strategy for planning and implementation.

The management tools include the systems approach, planning and problem-solving processes, and decision support systems. This chapter describes each of these and how they can be used effectively to implement both curriculum support services and library & information skills instruction. These tools and concepts provide the basis for the Six-Stage Strategy introduced at the end of the chapter.

• • •

THE SYSTEMS APPROACH

The systems approach can be described from two different (but related) perspectives.* One is based on context, the other on process. The first perspective concentrates on the contexts, broad and narrow, that comprise the framework for an entity (organization, person, institution) and is founded on the premise that "no one is an island." The same can be said of institutions, organizations and programs. These *systems* exist for some purpose and are composed of interacting components, some of which are systems themselves. In addition, a particular system (again, organization, institution, program) is usually part of some larger system.

---

* Much of the material on the systems approach as well as later material on rolling 5-year planning comes from class lectures and presentations by Evelyn Daniel, currently Dean of the School of Library Science, University of North Carolina at Chapel Hill. As there is nothing in print by Dean Daniel on these subjects, the authors are pleased to have the opportunity to present these ideas.

Systems and interrelationships among systems in education are as varied and complex as any in business or government. For example, an individual school may be considered a system (see figure 3.1). For this individual school, the immediate environment usually includes a school district, a community, and even broader, regional, state, and national social and political units.

More narrowly, the individual school may be composed of departments, service areas (e.g. guidance, special education, nurse), administrative entities, and of course, classes. Therefore, while the individual school may be viewed as a subsystem within a larger system, the school is also a system composed of a number of subsystems.

The building-level school media program exists within this individual school context. The media program interacts directly with other units within the school, with the subsystems vital to its operation, and with district and regional systems beyond the walls of the individual school.

Defining a program with a systems viewpoint is an important first step in planning and decision making because it provides an overall framework and structure. For the school library media specialist, a systems perspective can aid in setting goals and objectives, recognizing user populations and constituencies, and identifying external and internal sources of control, resource allocation, support and accountability. With regard to curriculum aspects of the media program, the very idea of providing curriculum support and integrating library & information skills with classroom content is based on a view of the library media program within a systems context.

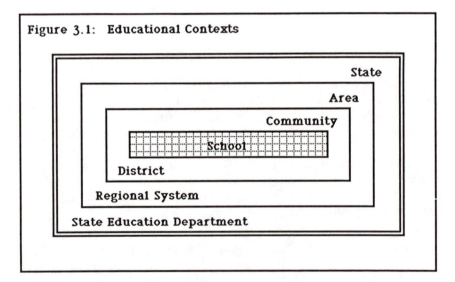

Figure 3.1. Educational Contexts

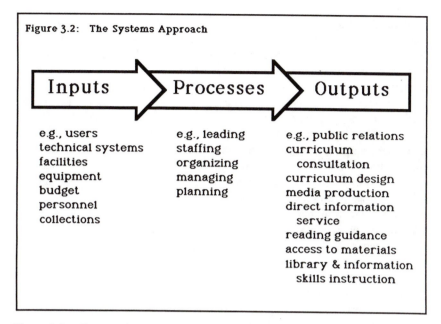

Figure 3.2:   The Systems Approach

Inputs	Processes	Outputs

e.g., users
technical systems
facilities
equipment
budget
personnel
collections

e.g., leading
staffing
organizing
managing
planning

e.g., public relations
curriculum
    consultation
curriculum design
media production
direct information
    service
reading guidance
access to materials
library & information
    skills instruction

Figure 3.2.   Systems Approach

As part of the planning process outlined later in this text, it is stressed that an *organizational information database* be set up. The purpose of this database is to provide documented facts about the structure (formal and informal, overt and hidden) of the individual school and broader units that interact with the library media program. It is argued that such a database is essential for proper planning and day-to-day operation of a curriculum-oriented media program. The information represented in the database is based on a systems perspective.

The second systems perspective concerns defining the flow and operation of a particular system as being represented by an *input - process - output model* (see figure 3.2).

Within the boundaries of a system, subsystems and components interact through *processes* to convert *input* (resources) to desired *output* (products, decisions, services). Too often, in examining or explaining a system, the focus tends to be on the input side. For example, the school library media program is often described in terms of numbers of books in the collection, floor space, seating capacity, budget, and size of staff. These *things* are essential to a functioning program but do not speak to the truly meaningful, creative aspects of the program. Program development, allocation of resources, and integrated curricula are not gained by stressing inputs. Rather, it is more appropriate and useful to consider a system first from the output side such as services provided.

Systems exist for some purpose. The output justifies the existence of the system. Defining goals and objectives is one way to focus on output. The purpose of a system is to create desired output through the processing of inputs. For school media programs, the primary goal is to provide services to constituencies: students, teachers, administration, community. It cannot be stressed too strongly that the services offered (output) justify the entire program. And today, the key library media services are those that relate to curriculum: (1) support services including resources provision, reading guidance, information service, curriculum consultation, and curriculum development; and (2) library & information skills instruction integrated with the subject area curriculum of the classroom. The question then is: How do you convert inputs to desired outputs?

The answer is *processes*. Processes are the activities that turn a collection of *things* into a meaningful program of services. Henri Fayol (1984), one of the founders of classical management theory, identifed the central management processes as planning, organizing, staffing, directing, and controlling.

Managers:

- plan what to accomplish;
- organize necessary resources;
- staff the organization with necessary personnel;
- direct the resources toward plan accomplishement;
- control the resources by comparing actual performance to the plan.

For the purposes of creating an effective program of library & information skills instruction and curriculum support services, the first and central process is planning.

PLANNING PROCESSES

As noted, processes are the mechanisms for converting inputs into desired outputs. A planning process consists of a series of steps deliberately taken to achieve objectives. There is no single, "correct" planning process; rather there are different approaches to the same end. For example Liesener (1976) designed a formal planning system based primarily on comparing desired outputs (services) to current services in light of existing and needed inputs (resources). The essential devices in Liesener's prescribed process are a series of instruments for surveying facts and opinion regarding the media program and reducing outputs and resources into costs (dollars) for comparative purposes.

Prostano and Prostano (1982) in their text on school library media management, outline *comprehensive planning* and decision making as a series of logical steps or stages. Their view, similar to the process designed by Liesener (1976) is that comprehensive planning consists of:

1. analyzing and evaluating the present condition of the program based on
    (a) external and internal constraints,
    (b) needs of users, and
    (c) comparison of the existing program to external standards, constraints, needs, and costs;
2. determining alternative objectives and programs based on findings;
3. securing approval for one or more alternatives; and
4. implementation.

Comprehensive planning refers to overall, global program planning. It is common to think of long-term comprehensive planning as a 3-year or 5-year plan. Evelyn Daniel champions a rolling 5-year plan.* A rolling 5-year plan begins with a detailed plan for year 1, and plans projecting four more years into the future with each year being less specific than the previous. It is "rolling" because at the end of year 1 there is again a projection five years into the future (with the original year 2 becoming year 1 and so on). The point is that planning is an ongoing process, requiring continuous re-evaluation and revision. A rolling plan does not imply never reaching one's goals. On the contrary, at any period, one should be able to look back to determine whether original activities, objectives, and goals were attained. More detail on 5-year plans is presented in chapter 7.

From the comprehensive plan, specific areas or subsystems can be targeted for more detailed planning. Ultimately, the concern is with *operational planning*: planning for the day-to-day delivery of services and instruction. Operational planning is short-term in scope, and oriented to implementation strategies and activities. Once established, operational plans are less flexible than more general plans. In a curriculum context, *unit* and *lesson plans* represent operational planning. Unit plans outline the major components of instruction, the general content, and time frame. Lesson plans provide information on the daily instructional activities and content.

TOP-DOWN PLANNING

Whether comprehensive or operational, planning should be top-down in nature. Major areas are first blocked out with broad strokes preceding penciling in details. Top-down planning involves plans within plans: master plans and subplans. After priorities and overall tasks are determined, details for each level can be spelled out. The converse of a top-down approach is a linear or sequential approach. Here, activities are taken in order, without consideration of priority or

---

* See earlier note.

modular components within components of tasks. While initially appealing in simplicity, linear planning often leads to unfinished projects.

Consider the typical library task of "cleaning up the card catalog." Most often the approach is sequential or linear: start with drawer A and work alphabetically from there. Unfortunately, most efforts rarely get beyond drawer B. Treating the problem from a top-down perspective might first involve a sampling of the catalog to determine problem areas. Then priorities are blocked out, and the activities to be completed determined. If, for example, the problem is found to be poor subject access, a top-down solution might be to first divide the catalog into separate subject and author-title drawers. Here again, before working with individual drawers, a top-down approach would call for a more systematic analysis of the actual problems.

Library & information skills instruction programs that start with orientation to the library media center and then work through specific sources are also using a sequential approach. Orientation *may* be an appropriate activity, but it seems more appropriate to review students' information needs first and then develop a systematic plan to teach the skills necessary to meet those needs, regardless of situation. This would reflect a top-down approach. The *Big Six Skills* curriculum outined in chapter 10 is based on a top-down assumption. In the Big Six Skills, the emphasis is on first developing an understanding of the overall information problem-solving process. Only then can areas for more specific skills development be tackled.

In planning for library & information skills instruction and curriculum support services, a top-down approach requires that comprehensive planning must precede strategic planning. Direction, focus, and priorities in instruction and support must be established before the development of specific unit and lesson plans.

A PROBLEM-SOLVING MODEL

The planning processes described above, as well as the Six-Stage Strategy for implementation of a curriculum support services and library & information skills program (outlined below and in chapters 4–7), are based on a general problem-solving methodology. While various versions of this methodology appear in the literature of management and education, Koberg and Bagnall, in *The Universal Traveler* (1980) describe the process with particular creativity.*

The first step in the Koberg and Bagnall model of the problem-solving process

---

* Figure 3.4 is from *The Universal Traveler, A Soft-Systems Guide to Creativity, Problem-Solving and the Process of Reaching Goals* by Don Koberg and Jim Bagnall. Copyright © 1980 by William Kaufmann, Inc., Los Altos, CA 94022. All rights reserved. The problem-solving terminology and figure3.3 are based on Koberg and Bagnall (1980). Used with permission.

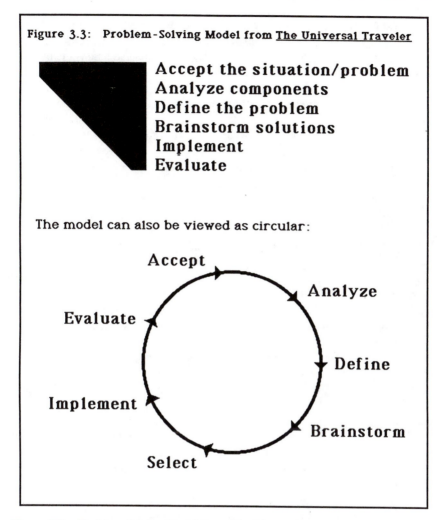

Figure 3.3:   Problem-Solving Model from The Universal Traveler

Accept the situation/problem
Analyze components
Define the problem
Brainstorm solutions
Implement
Evaluate

The model can also be viewed as circular:

Accept

Analyze

Evaluate

Define

Implement

Brainstorm

Select

Figure 3.3.   Problem-Solving Model from *The Universal Traveler*

is to *accept the situation/problem*. In some instances, the library media specialist may be wise to decide that certain problems are the province of others. For example, library media programs thrive in interdisciplinary environments. Consequently, in highly structured, departmentally organized schools, the structure itself is often viewed as limiting. This might be so, but is the tempting problem of changing the structure one that the library media specialist should tackle? Is it worth the tremendous effort? Is there a chance of success? The question here is not whether or not it is a problem, but rather, whether the library media specialist accepts it as an immediate problem.

Conversely, there are problems or situations which are forced on the library media specialist, such as a state-mandated library & information skills curriculum, overscheduling of classes, inferior budgets. In these situations the problem must be accepted and the methodology enacted.

After accepting a problem, the next steps are to *analyze the components* by gathering facts and opinions about the problem and then to accurately *define the problem*. These tasks are analogous to Prostanos' steps 1 & 2. Definition of the scope of a problem may be the most crucial part of the process. It is difficult to get somewhere without knowing the intended direction fairly specifically. Too often, library media specialists (and people in general) jump right into action in solving a problem without first spending the time to clarify the essential components, goals, and objectives. Goals are broad, general statements of purpose and represent an overall level at which to aim. Objectives are more specific indicators of what is to be achieved.

After defining the problem and before taking action, it is important to first consider alternative ways of achieving the objectives or solving the problem as defined. This consideration of options is best handled in two steps: *brainstorming* all possible alternatives (regardless of how farfetched some may appear) and *selecting the solution* that appears most likely to succeed. Only after carefully generating, evaluating and selecting an approach should the actual *implementation* take place.

Finally, too often, the problem-solving process ends with implementation. The crucial task of *evaluating* whether or not a problem was adequately solved is often omitted or left incomplete. This is true in spite of the fact that the problem-solving process (and most planning systems) are based on the assumption that rethinking and revision will be necessary follow-up activities. This is particularly true for curriculum-related problems and situations. School curriculum is not static; the needs of students and teachers are constantly changing. Evaluation and modification of existing program elements are essential for quality curriculum support. Skills instruction programs and library media support services need to be continually evaluated in light of changing classroom content.

While the problem-solving process has been described in sequence, it need not be so. Quite often, the result of a particular step will require reconsideration at a prior level (see figure 3.4). For example, analysis and definition may result in reconsidering whether to accept the situation or not; the selection phase may be unsatisfactory, thus requiring generation of new alternatives; or evaluation may determine that the solution selected was not properly implemented. This *feedback* in the process is reasonable and should be encouraged. Finally, one way to view the entire process is circular: as one problem is resolved, another begins (see figure 3.3).

Again, regarding problem-solving and planning, a top-down approach is recommended. This is to avoid getting caught up with time-consuming details when broad problems exist.

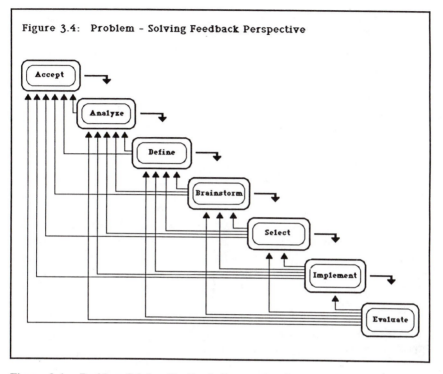

Figure 3.4:   Problem – Solving Feedback Perspective

Figure 3.4.   Problem-Solving Feedback Perspective from *The Universal Traveler*

SUPPORT SYSTEMS

The concept of support systems comes from the field of management. *Decision support systems* developed as an alternative to the ambitious attempts to meet the global information needs of an organization through large-scale management information systems (MIS). While valuable for storing, accessing, and manipulating major databases (e.g., personnel or client records in a corporation), MIS has proved unable to provide the kind of customized, small-scale, information support needed in many decision-making situations.

Decision support systems (DSS), human or informational, are intended to assist managers in solving problems and working toward stated goals. They should be designed to be flexible, adaptable, and geared to specific problems. DSS represents a type of information system, locally controlled, which helps improve the effectiveness of organizations and the people who work in them. (Sprague,1980). "A DSS must produce information in a form managers understand, when such information is needed, and under their direct control" (Carlson 1977). Decision support systems should provide information and support for carrying out the management processes noted above.

For the purposes of designing and implementing the curriculum-related portion of the library media program (integrated library & information skills instruction and curriculum support services), it is recommended that seven decision support systems be considered:

1.   System-level planning group;
2.   Building-level planning group;
3.   Library media specialist support group;
4.   Organizational information file;
5.   Curriculum database;
6.   Library & information skills curriculum;
7.   Curriculum support services checklist.

The first three systems are people-oriented, while the last four are informational in nature. Each meets an identified need in the Six-Stage Strategy. Together they comprise the human and information support necessary for successful curriculum program development and implementation. Each of the seven support systems is explained in more detail in chapter 5.

A STRATEGY FOR IMPLEMENTING CURRICULUM-RELATED FUNTIONS OF THE LIBRARY MEDIA PROGRAM

In the next four chapters, a sequence of stages is presented specifically aimed at implementing, (1) a program of curriculum support services and, (2) a library & information skills curriculum integrated with subject area, classroom instruction. The stages are based on the general model outlined above but include analysis and planning instruments particularly appropriate for curriculum-related program development. The steps of the *Six-Stage Strategy* are:

1.   *Review existing situation*: Gather information about the current state of affairs and analyze that information;
2.   *Define goals and objectives*: Based on the local situation, articulate desired outcomes;
3.   *Set up support systems*: Create and maintain human and information resources for decision-making;
4.   *Conduct feasibility analysis*: Determine what is possible given stated objectives and reality;
5.   *Develop plans*: Based upon objectives and the feasibility analysis, articulate what is to occur and when;
6.   *Evaluate plans and processes*: Determine the viability of the plans and the effectiveness of the strategy.

Implementation is omitted from specific reference in the strategy because it is the ultimate goal of the process. The entire purpose of the process is to develop plans and guidelines for implementation. In addition, implementation also involves carrying out the activities noted in each stage. Therefore, implementation is inherent to the entire strategy.

SUMMARY

This chapter has provided information on management techniques particularly appropriate for the development, implementation, and evaluation of curriculum-related aspects of the library media program. While the techniques outlined have value beyond curriculum concerns and library media programs, the major concern of this book is with curriculum-related, library media functions. To this end, the Six-Stage Strategy represents a specific, practical approach to curriculum concerns. The next four chapters look more closely at each step, and how the steps interact.

PART II

THE SIX-STAGE STRATEGY FOR LIBRARY MEDIA CURRICULUM PROGRAM DEVELOPMENT AND MANAGEMENT

This part offers a systematic planning strategy to developing the two major curriculum-related functions of the library media program: (1) curriculum support services, and (2) instruction in library & information skills. The objectives of the section are to:

- explain the nature and purpose of the Six-Stage Strategy;
- understand the requirements and components of the stages in the process;
- use the Six-Stage Strategy for implementing a curriculum services program and library & information skills program;
- evaluate the effectiveness of the Six-Stage Strategy in implementing a curriculum services and library & information skills instruction program.

Curriculum support services are integral to the implementation of a school's curriculum. Library & information skills instruction address the needs of students in an information-rich society. These two major functions of the overall library program are naturally linked due to their common relationship to the overall school curriculum. Curriculum support requires a knowledge of what is really going on in classrooms, overall curriculum goals and objectives, and a good working relationship with teachers and administrators. Similarly, in order to effectively implement an integrated library & information skills program, the library media specialist must know the classroom curriculum, the overall curriculum, and be able to work closely with teachers and administrators. Based on the more general problem solving methodology noted in chapter two, the *Six-Stage Strategy* is suggested for implementing both a curriculum support services and library & information skills program.

Adopting a systematic strategy can be the key to meeting the challenge of curriculum functions. It is easy to get caught up in the day-to-day needs of library media program users as well as managing the various collections and technical systems of the physical library media center. However, to be effective in the long run, the library media specialist must step back and systematically review where the program is, where it should be, and decide how to get there. This is the essence of the Six-Stage Strategy:

1. Review existing situation
2. Define goals and objectives
3. Set up support systems
4. Conduct feasibility analysis
5. Develop plans
6. Evaluate plans and processes

While presented in a linear fashion, the strategy is not necessarily linear. It is often necessary and desirable to back up, revise, and gather additional information. This branching or feedback in the process should not be seen as a problem, but rather as further refinement of the program. In fact, it may be useful to view the general flow of the strategy as a cycle of information gathering, analysis, planning, and evaluation.

The Six-Stage Strategy is explained in detail in chapters 4 - 7. Each stage of the strategy is outlined in terms of components, necessary tasks, tools and approaches, and the relationship of the stage to other stages in the strategy.

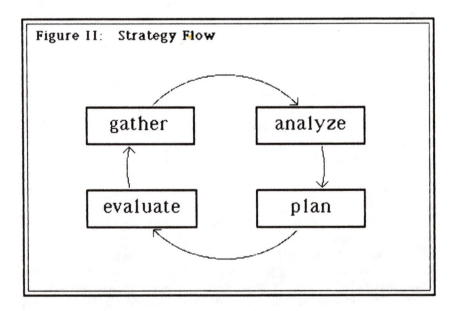

Figure II: Strategy Flow

Figure II. Strategy Flow

CHAPTER 4

The Six-Stage Strategy:

| Review Situation | Goals and Objectives | Support Systems | Feasibility Analysis | Develop Plans | Evaluate Plans |

Stage 1: Review existing situation

Stage 2: Define goals and objectives

This chapter focuses on the first two stages of the six stage strategy. Stage 1, review existing situation, is a necessary prerequisite to planning and program development. It requires gathering information about the current state of affairs. Once this has been determined and documented, it is possible to conduct stage 2: the definition of goals and objectives for both curriculum support services and integrated library & information skills instruction.

STAGE 1: REVIEW EXISTING SITUATION

Before any effort is made to change existing (or establish new) curriculum-related library media program activities, it is first necessary to determine the current state of affairs. This is true whether it is an existing setting with which the library media specialist is intimately familiar or an entirely new situation. The aim of the review stage is to take stock, determine the parameters of the situation, and develop a general framework for the stages to come.

As noted, the review stage is informational in nature. It is suggested that information be gathered on:

1. the current state of library media program involvement in curriculum support and skills instruction,
2. curriculum mandates, requirements, and general needs,
3. local and state standards,

4.   general attitudes of students, teachers, and administrators toward the library media program,
5.   support elements (inputs) of the library media program,
6.   anticipated future developments.

The information requirements of the review stage can also be considered as answers to a series of questions:

1.   What is the general, current level of involvement of the library media program in curriculum and instruction? In curriculum development?
2.   Are there specific curriculum mandates related to the library media program?
3.   What general curriculum support services does the library media program offer to students, teachers, and administrators?
4.   Are there local and regional standards? Are they considered in library media program development and support?
5.   How do students, teachers, and administrators perceive the library media program?
6.   What is the general state of support (i.e., input elements) for the library media program?
7.   What are the personal strengths and interests of library media personnel?
8.   Who are the key "players" at the building, district, and regional level?
9.   Is the general school situation stable? Are there likely to be major changes in structure, program, or personnel in the near future?

Through these types of questions, general information about the existing environment can be compiled. The overall intent in stage 1 is to gain a general perspective on the current situation and provide a basis for setting goals and objectives. More detailed, exhaustive information will be systematically gathered and documented in stage 3.

STAGE 2: DEFINE GOALS AND OBJECTIVES

The general information gathered above provides the basis for stage 2, the articulation of goals and objectives for the library media program in the curriculum support services and skills instruction areas. *Goals* are broad, general statements of purpose and represent an overall level at which to aim. *Objectives* are more specific indicators of what is to be achieved. Collectively, the goals and objectives should articulate what is exactly desired.

In defining goals and objectives, there needs to be a consideration of the nature of the local situation, the needs of students and teachers, state and local mandates, standards, and interests of library media personnel. Again, this information should be available from stage 1. If not, it may be necessary to back up and collect missing information.

The reality of the existing situation should be recognized but not overly restrictive in setting goals and objectives. There needs to be a balance between what exists and what is desired. If one is to err, let it be on the side of aiming too high. At the same time, totally unrealistic goals and objectives are easily dismissed as unattainable. A good rule-of-thumb might be to plan for what seems possible and then push up the expectations just a bit.

While goals and objectives should be tailored to local needs, there is much common ground across programs. What often differs is the scope and depth of involvement. These differences are often the result of limited resources, support, and/or the abilities of library media personnel. Again, the current state of affairs is the basis for goal-setting, but should not be taken as fixed and unalterable.

Some examples of goals related to the curriculum concerns of the library media program include:

- meeting the information needs of students related to research;
- providing direct information service;
- providing materials (print and nonprint) support for classroom instruction;
- providing access to resources beyond the library media center;
- having teachers understand the role of the library media program in curriculum development and implementation;
- being involved in the school's curriculum development process; and
- teaching students basic information skills.

As noted, objectives are more specific statements about the library media program's role in curriculum. Objectives articulate how goals are to be specifically attained. There are both short-term and long-term objectives.

Some examples of objectives are:

- work with one unit from each major subject area during this year;
- develop one library & information skills subject area unit in each grade level in each of the next five years;
- provide one literature appreciation activity to each class each month;
- teach the research and information problem-solving process to all tenth grade students;
- have all students understand the Big Six library and information skills;
- provide a current awareness service to third grade teachers;
- become a member of the school's curriculum committee;
- run an in-service workshop for teachers on the library & information skills curriculum and the integrated approach;
- provide resource stations in the library media center for specific class projects;

- participate in school library media networks; and
- be available for answering reference questions.

Writing goals and objectives is not an easy task, particularly if attempted by one person. It is more advantageous to work with teachers and administrators in a committee or group. A group approach provides a range of input, adds credibility to the goals and objectives, facilitates communication to others, and builds support for the library media program.

If a building or district level planning group does not exist, it may be desirable to set one up before completely defining goals and objectives. Planning groups are included in the support systems listed in stage 3. It may be advantageous to establish a planning group before completing the definition stage. This would be an example of branching to a later stage and then returning to complete the tasks of the earlier stage. In certain situations this may be appropriate; in others, unnecessary or not feasible. While certainly a potentially valuable asset, the establishment of a planning group should not be viewed as a prerequisite to defining goals and objectives.

Lastly, the statement of goals and objectives doesn't have to be considered in a formal, permanent context. In lieu of prior statements of direction, a rough sketch of what the program is attempting to accomplish is a reasonable first effort.

●　●　●

The explanation of the Six-Stage Strategy continues in the next chapter with a discussion of support systems. Those support systems particularly useful for library media program development are identified and explained.

CHAPTER 5

The Six-Stage Strategy:

Review Situation	Goals and Objectives	**Support Systems**	Feasibility Analysis	Develop Plans	Evaluate Plans

Stage 3: Set Up Support Systems

In the Six-Stage Strategy, after initial goals and objectives are set, the next requirement is for more detailed, accurate information on specific elements of the situation. Stage 3 approaches this problem through  **establishing support systems. The** concept of decision support systems was introduced in chapter 3. DSS refers to setting up and maintaining human and information resources valuable for program development and decision making. This chapter describes seven support systems found to be particularly useful in developing quality curriculum-related aspects of library media programs.

• • •

The existence of permanent support systems will greatly enhance the library media specialist's ability to carry out program planning, design, and implementation. In addition, support systems usually aid and encourage administrators and others concerned with management, program development, and decision making beyond the library media program.

Support systems are designed to document reality and provide reliable information on the existing state of affairs. Support systems are conceived as ongoing efforts. Once established, support systems are the backbone of planning and implementation activities. Finally, support systems are intended to be local in nature. The ideas presented should be adapted and customized to local needs.

Support systems can be a database, available computer system, human network, or commissioned report. For curriculum concerns of the library media program, seven human and information support systems have been identified as particularly useful:

Human support systems:

1. District (system-level) planning group
2. Local (building-level) planning group

3. Library media professional support group

Information support systems:

4. Organizational information file
5. Curriculum database
6. Library & information skills curriculum
7. Curriculum support services checklist

HUMAN SUPPORT SYSTEMS

The first set of support systems may already exist to some degree. These are the *people-based* committees and groups set up to guide and advise the library media program.

1. The District (System-Level) Planning Group

This group provides overall coordination of efforts. Its purpose is to insure consistency and continuity within a district and in relation to state or regional requirements. In addition to coordinating with other programs on the district level, this group can mandate on a district level if necessary and recommend resource (financial and staff) allocations. An effective district planning group is composed of representatives from faculty, administration, and the library media program.

2. The Local (Building-Level) Planning Group

The local planning group performs a similar function but on the individual school level. It too serves to guide and advise the library media program and coordinate it with the overall instructional program in the school. The building-level planning group provides credibility and support on a local level. Composed of teachers across grade levels and/or subjects (as appropriate), administrator(s), and library media personnel, it can facilitate local implementation through: (1) identifying local needs, (2) setting realistic goals, (3) gaining the cooperation of faculty and administration, and (4) making recommendations for resource allocation on the local level. The library media specialist should consider the local planning group as an advisory council, providing a forum for consultation and assistance on problem areas.

3. The Library Media Professional Support Group

The last human support system is the library media professional support group. This group brings together library media people who are involved in similar situations. The purpose is to break down their feeling of isolation. This group can be coordinated through professional associations, regional networks, or other already existing structures. While there may be district-wide library media committees, it is suggested that this group be broad enough to bring in differing views and approaches. Conversely, it is important that the group be convenient and small enough so that participants feel comfortable and able to share ideas, information and problems.

INFORMATION SUPPORT SYSTEMS

The next set of support systems are informational in nature. It is less likely that these already exist in some systematic form. As information professionals in the school, library media specialists can provide a service to themselves as well as teachers and administrators by setting up these or similar information support systems. Three specific support systems are noted below. These are viewed as minimal for successful creation of a quality curriculum support services and integrated skills instruction program. In a local situation, it may be desireable to have additional information support systems.

4. The Organizational Information File

The organizational information file provides documentation on the organizational framework of the school. As a foundation for development and implementation of a curriculum support services and library & information skills program, the availability of accurate, documented building level information is crucial. Based on the systems approach described in chapter 3, there also needs to be an awareness of surrounding environments (systems)—district, region, state—that affect the local situation. Therefore, in addition to the information listed below, this support system will include information on the district situation and beyond.

If all this information has not been collected, it is appropriate for the library media specialist, acting as information manager, to gather and evaluate information about:

- the organization of students (groupings, scheduling);
- the structure of instruction (e.g. self-contained classes, teams, etc.);
- the scheduling of classes;
- a typical teacher's day;
- the administrative arrangement (e.g. are there department heads?—assistants to the principal?—district level subject area coordinators?);
- the structure and organization of curriculum;
- access to the library media center (open, scheduled, passes).

Figure 5.1.   An example of an organization structure for a school

☐   A three grade middle school, grades 6-8.
☐   Students grouped into classes, 20-30 per class.
☐   435 students in the school.
☐   Major subject areas (English, social studies, science, math) are organized in teams, three teams per grade level.
☐   Special subjects are art, music, physical education, home economics, foreign language, and industrial arts.
☐   Most subjects are taught daily; Art and music are half year courses
☐   Curriculum in each subject is organized by units.
☐   The library media center is open-access; requires passes from lunch and study hall.
☐   The library media program has a required library & information skills component.
☐   There is one principal and designated team leaders.

This type of information is dynamic; it must be updated periodically. The overall development and management of a library media program should fit the framework of the school. While some organizational structures are more suited to effective library media programming than others, changing a long-standing structure is a difficult task and chances of success are small. It may be possible and worth the effort to change structures that directly affect the library media program (for example, a full schedule of classes in the library media center or study halls in the library media center). But efforts to change the structure on a broader level are probably not effective uses of time and effort.

5. The Curriculum Database

As stressed previously, curriculum is at the heart of the educational process. Accurate, up-to-date information on curriculum is essential to effective support services and integrated skills instruction. Curriculum information is the foundation for library media programming as well as for general planning in the school.

The basic building block of curriculum is the *curriculum unit*. Therefore, minimally, curriculum information should be available on the general scope and sequence of units:

1. for each grade
2. in each subject area
3. for each teacher.

Generally, the most available source of curriculum information is the *curricu-*

lum guide, a locally or regionally produced document outlining the required or recommended course of study. While these district or state curriculum guides are useful and should be collected and maintained, they often do not represent the curriculum as actually carried out in a school. Fenwick English (1978) has referred to curriculum guides as the "fictional curriculum." Library media specialists need "nonfiction" information on the curriculum in order to note units requiring support or development and/or those units particularly appropriate for integrating with library & information skills instruction. A file or database of *real* curriculum information, on the components of curriculum units, is vital for planning and implementation.

In most instances, *real* information on the curriculum is not readily available. Some method of systematically gathering and evaluating information on what is actually going on in the classroom must be undertaken by the library media specialist in cooperation with the building administration and teaching staff. An effective means for collecting, storing, and presenting information on curriculum is *curriculum mapping*, developed by Fenwick English (1978, 1979, 1980). Eisenberg (1984) has documented the effectiveness of using curriculum mapping in library media contexts.

The process of building the curriculum database through curriculum mapping is explained in detail in chapter 8.

6. The Library & Information Skills Curriculum

Today it is widely accepted that certain skills and concepts relating to the access, use, and presentation of information are vital components of a student's education. The articulation and suggested scope and sequence for those skills are outlined in a library & information skills curriculum. As with other curriculum guides, the library & information skills curriculum does not represent reality in terms of the actual instruction and learning taking place in a school. Rather, the curriculum outline should serve as a guide to those library & information skills deemed important as content components in the school's instructional program.

It is not necessary or recommended that each library media specialist or even district create his or her own scope and sequence of skills. Many reasonable outlines already exist.*

A different approach to a library & information skills curriculum is presented in this book. Developed from a *critical thinking skills* perspective, the *Big Six Skills* curriculum is based on Bloom's (1956) taxonomy of objectives in the cognitive domain.** In addition, rather than dealing with specific resources or

---

* Walker and Montgomery (second ed., 1983), Wehmeyer (second ed., 1984) offer library media skills curricula. The curricula of a number of states including Hawaii 1979, Maine 1984, North Carolina 1985, and New York 1980, 1986 are available in the ERIC database.

** Bloom's taxonomy and the information problem-solving approach to the library & information skills curriculum are explained in detail in chapter 10.

library systems, the emphasis is on developing broad skills areas reflecting the *information problem-solving process*. Thus, the curriculum can be easily summarized in terms of the *Big Six Skills*:

task definition
information-seeking strategies
location and access
use of information
synthesis
evaluation

More detailed, specific objectives are noted within each of these Big Six Skills. In addition to being information-based (not just source- or library- based), the curriculum recognizes: (1) skill development with the full range of library media materials, (2) reading guidance, literacy and literature-related aspects, and (3) computer skills. See chapter 10 for a full explanation of the approach and the actual scope and sequence.

In terms of the overall *Six-Stage Strategy* and creation of support systems, it is not necessary to adopt this particular library & information skills curriculum. Rather, it is recommended that existing library & information skills curriculum outlines be reviewed in relation to local needs, and that one be chosen, revised and adapted to the local situation. In doing this, certain general guidelines are suggested:

(a) Integrate skills with the classroom content.   Why is it that high school and college librarians decry the lack of ability on the part of students to use basic library tools (the classic example being the card catalog) when these same students have been instructed in library use since the third grade? It is because library & information skills instruction should not take place in a vacuum. While it is certainly possible to teach library & information skills in separate *library classes* (with accompanying lesson plans, teaching aids and props, quizzes and tests), these efforts are generally doomed to failure. Students best make the connection between learned skills and *real world* situations when they are required to use those skills for *real purposes*. While the library media program is responsible for coordination and implementation of the curriculum, the direct teaching of library & information skills is not the sole responsibility of the library media professional. Library & information skills are integrally related to the information needs of students, and should be integrally tied to the content, activities, and processes of the classroom. This is a central and uncompromising assumption to many current skills curricula and basic to the Six-Stage Strategy.

(b) Use a top-down approach.   Broad, general information skills, related to the information problem-solving process, should be stressed before dealing with detailed, specific sources or library systems. Students need to develop an understanding of why they need information and how information-seeking and use fits

into a more general process *before* learning specific sources or even where things are located in the library media center. Without the overview, the specifics are meaningless. This top-down approach provides students with both a context for and a powerful approach to meeting information problems. Furthermore, for those library media programs with limited time and resources, this approach offers an organized, systematic way of making compromises in instruction without sacrificing overall, essential aspects because a top-down approach stresses the important concepts not the trivial.

(c) Be realistic but think big.   The effectiveness and scope of a library & information skills curriculum and instruction is naturally limited by the support elements of the overall library media program. Obviously the most crucial support items are staff time and collections. Therefore, while every library media program must meet responsibilities in skills instruction, the level of program development will vary from school to school. As explained, a top-down approach can be valuable in developing a program within given limits. At the same time, library media specialists are encouraged to think beyond the status quo. Library & information skills instruction cuts across all subject areas. By actively demonstrating the value of information and library & information skills in achieving classroom objectives, library media programs gain status. Growth and increased resource allocation often follow. Conversely, programs rarely expand by accommodating to limited resources.

(d) Don't forget the other aspects of the program.   Library & information skills instruction is only one component of the overall library media program. Reading guidance, access to materials, media production services, and curriculum support services are important to meeting the library and information needs of students and faculty. Therefore development and planning must balance the skills curriculum with other output elements of the library media program. One approach is to recognize and promote these components within the library & information skills curriculum.

7. Curriculum Support Services Checklist

The phrase *curriculum support* has traditionally referred to those services involved with making library materials available to teachers and students. This book is concerned with a much broader and more active view of curriculum support services. If the library media program is truly integral to the entire curriculum, library media specialists must directly contribute in a range of service areas. Therefore, in this book, the phrase *curriculum support services* implies a great deal more including:

* curriculum design and development;
* evaluation of curriculum (from an information use perspective);

- guidance in selection of reading materials;
- production of print, audio, video, and computer materials;
- design, development, and delivery of enrichment programs (for example,
- special activities in literature appreciation, media, storytelling, humanities, science, etc.);
- interpretation of curriculum (e.g. assignments) for students;
- design and development of instructional materials; as well as the traditional
- provision of space, materials and equipment.

In this book, curriculum support services are grouped into five major areas:

1. resources provision (RP);
2. reading guidance (RG);
3. information service (IS);
4. curriculum consulation (CC); and
5. curriculum development (CD).

Examples of specific curriculum support services associated with these general areas include: serving on a district curriculum committee (curriculum development); consultation with individual teachers on assignments (curriculum consultation); providing current awareness services to administrators (information service); working on a special "authors in the schools" activity (reading guidance); and putting together a collection for a classroom of materials on birds of the Northeast (resources provision).

Each individual library media program should offer a range of specific curriculum support services within each of the five areas. These should meet local needs and should be listed in a locally created *curriculum support services checklist*. This checklist documents those curriculum support services presently offered and provides the basis for planning new support activities. Too often, curriculum support services are offered in an ad-hoc, haphazard manner. A documented, publicized curriculum support services checklist facilitates a systematic approach to curriculum support. In addition, it increases awareness of the full range of services offered and serves to raise the status of these essential activities in the eyes of teachers and administrators. Chapter 9 outlines the curriculum support services function in more detail and offers additional suggestions for a curriculum services checklist.

SUMMARY

The seven support systems described above are those identified as valuable for planning, implementing, and managing curriculum-related library media functions. By definition, support systems are locally created and customized to meet local needs. It should be apparent that not all of these support systems need to be created from scratch. Some will already be in place; others will simply require modifications. There is no need (nor desire) to "reinvent the wheel." Whenever possible, identify, collect and use existing structures and resources. Support systems do need to be in place in order to carry out the last three stages of the strategy.

CHAPTER 6

The Six-Stage Strategy:

| Review Situation | Goals and Objectives | Support Systems | Feasibility Analysis | Develop Plans | Evaluate Plans |

Stage 4: Conduct Feasibility Analysis

The purpose of the **feasibility analysis** stage is to determine what is possible given what is desired and what is available. Here, goals and reality collide, and what is left forms the basis of the plans to follow. This chapter discusses feasibility from two perspectives: program and resources.

Based on the systems model (input—process—output), there are actually two parts to the feasibility analysis: *program feasibility* and *resources feasibility*. Program feasibility analysis is concerned with determining what is possible and desirable on the *output* side. Based on the school curriculum, library & information skills curriculum, and curriculum support services, what is feasible in terms of program? Where do the classroom and library media center most obviously intersect? For skills instruction, which classroom units are most appropriate for integration? For curriculum support services, where are the areas most in need of services? What is currently being done, and where are the deficiencies? What are the priorities?

In addition, at some point it is necessary to consider what is feasible from an *input* or resources perspective. That is, beyond program concerns, what are reasonable expectations given the present state of staffing, collections, systems, facilities, and cooperation of teachers and administrators? Conversely, what increases in resources will be necessary to attain full program objectives? The resources feasibility stage documents what is possible given anticipated levels of resources as well what can be expected if current levels are increased. Library media programs should not be totally constrained by present resource allocations. At the same time, unrealistic program projections based on false expectations on the resource side can only lead to failure.

43

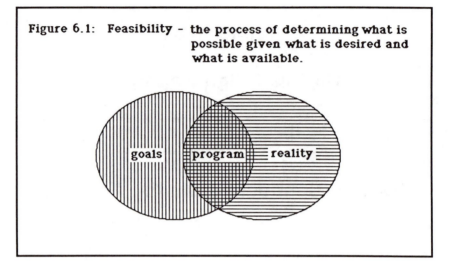

Figure 6.1:   Feasibility – the process of determining what is
               possible given what is desired and
               what is available.

Figure 6.1.   Feasibility

PROGRAM FEASIBILITY

The overriding task in determining what is feasible from a program perspective is to bring the curriculum-related objectives of the library media program together with the reality of the existing school curriculum. The guiding curriculum goals and objectives of the library media program were established in stage 2. In addition, these goals and objectives are articulated operationally in (1) the library & information skills curriculum and (2) the curriculum support services checklist. Curriculum information about what is actually going on in classrooms is provided by curriculum mapping. Fundamentally, program feasibiltiy analysis requires reviewing curriculum mapping information to determine those units most appropriate for library & information skills instruction and curriculum support services.

The following procedure is suggested for determining program feasibility:

(a)   Review goals and objectives. Establish priorities and major needs to be addressed.
(b)   Review the library & information skills curriculum. From a top-down perspective, establish scope and priorities.
(c)   Review the curriculum support services checklist. Determine those services already in place and the requirements for initiating others. Establish priorities.
(d)   Review the curriculum maps. This step is the heart of program feasibility analysis.

From the perspective of *library & information skills instruction*, the task is to identify units that are most appropriate for skills integration. Curriculum maps provide information about units regarding:

- Duration of instruction (time);
- Level of instruction;
- Teaching methods;
- Materials used in instruction;
- Organization of instruction; and
- Evaluation.

In general, units most appropriate for library & information skills instruction have one or more of the following characteristics:

- a major unit, central to the overall curriculum;
- of comparatively long duration;
- reinforce or expand on basic concepts and skills;
- use a combination of teaching methods;
- require multiple, nontext sources;
- organize instruction in a number of different ways;
- evaluate performance in ways other than tests.

For example, contrast these two units for appropriateness for integration with library & information skills instruction:

- a science unit on weather, averaging three periods a week for six weeks, using multiple, nontext sources and a combination of teaching methods, with full class lectures as well as students working in small groups or individually, final evaluation based on a report and experiments;
- an English unit on parts of a sentence, lasting two weeks, relying on a textbook, taught by lecture and class discussion, evaluated by a test.

Clearly, the library media program should focus on the science unit.

Feasibility in integrated skills instruction also needs to be concerned with proper scheduling and subject diversity. That is, integrated instructional units should not all take place during the same months or quarter. Nor should they just involve certain subject areas, such as English and social studies. Interdisciplinary units are particularly suited to library & information skills instruction. Again, comparing objectives to curriculum maps can aid in this kind of feasibility determination.

Looking at the curriculum maps from a *curriculum support services* perspective, the key questions are:

- Which are the significant units in each grade level? In each subject area? Has the library media program been involved in designing these units?
- Which units require multiple nontext materials? Is the library media program meeting these needs?
- Which units use one source (nontext) materials? Is the library media program assisting in selecting and evaluating these materials?
- Which units require a product, paper, or report as an evaluation method? Is the library media program involved in these units?

These questions will point to those units most in need of and appropriate for curriculum support services. For example, those units relying on multiple non-text materials have an obvious need for library media support services. If the library media program is not involved in supporting these units, why not? How are the units' needs being met? If the library media program is involved, what is the level and extent of support services? Are there opportunities for further development or expansion of services?

Of course, every unit in the curriculum has some information component. Theoretically, the library media program could be involved to some degree in every unit. Realistically, library media professionals must set priorities. This is the next task.

(e)   Analyze the identified units and set priorities.

After the library & information skills curriculum and curriculum support services have been reviewed (steps 2 and 3 above), and the curriculum has been analyzed to identify key units (step 4), it is time to put the library media program and school's curriculum together and set priorities.

Again, the top-down approach should be a guide in making choices. Those units most promising in terms of integration with skills instruction or most in need of support services should be handled first. The less promising units have a lower priority and can be dealt with as time permits.

Some guidelines in determining priorities include:

- the match between elements of the library & information skills curriculum (the Big Six Skills) and identified classroom units;
- the match between curriculum support services and identified units;
- the scope and depth of library & information skills to be covered;
- the major units in each grade;
- the major units in each subject area;
- units that are common to a number of teachers.

The priority-setting process is a give-and-take, thinking and rethinking activity. It often requires going back to the curriculum maps, skills curriculum, and services checklist. Consultation with teachers and administrators is also important in reviewing choices and establishing priorities.

(f)   Document decisions and priorities.

The final result of program feasibility should be a priority listing of units with associated library & information skills and curriculum support services. This listing may be considered as the beginning of stage 5 (planning) in the overall Six-Stage Strategy. The listing is a first-draft, a rough outline of priorities and will likely change due to scheduling, changing requirements, unanticipated problems, and of course, availability of resources.

RESOURCES FEASIBILITY

At some point, beyond program, it is necessary to consider what is feasible given the reality of the existing situation. Here, the curriculum-related functions of skills instruction and curriculum support services are tied to levels of available or forthcoming resources. In resources feasibility analysis, desired outputs are linked to given inputs. Rather than a negative experience, this step should be viewed as an opportunity to clearly state what is possible given current resources *as well as* what can be expected if resource levels are increased. It also places the potentially unpleasant task of setting limits in a broader, more objective context. The burden of making difficult choices becomes a school-wide problem as the relationship between program activities and resources is made clear to those administrators (or school board members) responsible for resource allocation. If resources are increased, the library media program is in a position to increase outputs. Likewise, cuts in resources will necessitate cuts in program.

The major resources to consider are:

- professional staff time
- support staff time
- collections
- equipment
- technical systems
- facilities
- cooperation of others
- flexibility

The most crucial resource or input item is *time*: professional time and support staff time. More than anything else, the amount of professional time determines what is possible in terms of curriculum support services and library & information skills instruction. Periodic review is advisable to determine (1) where pro-

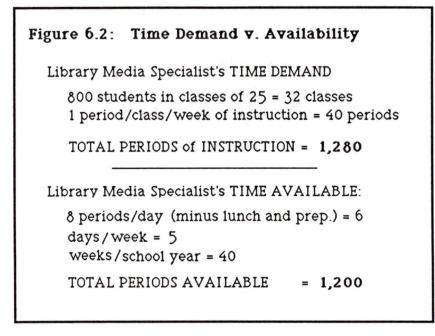

Figure 6.2. Time Demand v. Availability

fessional and staff time are actually being spent, and (2) whether these are the tasks and activities that are considered priority areas.*

Both theory and reality refute the notion that library media specialists are directly responsible for teaching *all* classes relating to library & information skills instruction. Skills instruction is best accomplished when integrated with classroom content and is the joint responsibility of library media specialists and teachers. The library media specialist is, however, responsible for overall coordination and development of the curriculum as well as documenting how library & information skills objectives are met.

For example, the Regents Action Plan recently implemented in the state of New York (New York State Education Department 1984) calls for the equivalent of "one period per week in library skills instruction" (40 periods per year) for all seventh and eighth grade students. Even if library media specialists accepted this mandate as their sole responsibility, they could not possibly meet the demands (see figure 6.2).

Fortunately the designers of the New York State Regents Action Plan recognize this fact. It is expressly stated in the curriculum that skills are to be taught by library media specialists *and* classroom teachers. Furthermore, library & infor-

---

* A time-management study can be revealing and useful in analyzing professional and support staff time. Appendix B explains how to conduct a time-management study.

mation skills instruction should not be integrated with just one or two subject areas, but rather should involve a full range of subjects.

Overall, library media specialists and support staff (aides, secretaries, assistants) need to spend significant time in service, consultation, and instruction areas. Of course, if the staffing situation is seriously below *minimal* standards (minimally there should be one library media specialist and one aide for a school with 800 students), expectations in the level of services provided must also be lowered.

Available resources determine the extent of program involvement. At the same time, library media specialists in less than desirable situations must work toward increasing the level of resource allocation. This is part of the comprehensive five-year planning process. A start in this process would be the systematic documentation and reporting to administrators and teachers of what the situation is, the compromises that have been made, and the potential program that could be offered given adequate resources. As noted in chapter 3, the focus needs to be first on output objectives (that is, the provision of curriculum support services and skills instruction) and second, on the necessary staff and resources to meet stated objectives.*

An examination of feasibility from a resource perspective leads to a realization that a library media specialist can be involved in about two or three periods per day of direct skills instruction and that others need to be involved in teaching skills. Again, those library media specialists in totally locked-in, scheduled situations need to start building a case for more flexibility while determining what realistic improvements are possible within the scheduled class structure. The program feasibility has identified and prioritized major units. Resource feasibility determines which units will be dealt with and the time to be spent on them. Other scheduled periods should be designed to be less demanding on the library media specialist (for example, use films, video, or other *canned* activities).

Collections, equipment, technical systems, and facilities are also important considerations in determining what is feasible. For example, if skills instruction focuses on a topic as progressive as online searching of the ERIC database, the periodicals collection (or interlibrary loan) must be able to provide a reasonable number of the journal articles students are going to want. Similarly, if the physical facility cannot accommodate a full class for instruction purposes, direct teaching by the library media specialist had better occur in the classroom.

---

* A full discussion of how to deal with limited resources as well as systematic, comprehensive planning to increase allocations is beyond the scope of this book. The need for resources documented in the feasibility analysis becomes part of the overall plan. Library media specialists are encouraged not to accept the status quo in poorly supported situations and to work systematically to increase resource allocations. Liesener (1976) and Prostano and Prostano (1982) are just two of many texts that provide systematic approaches to comprehensive planning.

Finally, while it may seem unusual to list cooperation as a resource, without the active support and participation of teachers, administrators, students, and community, the planning and implementation of an effective program is severely handicapped. As noted in chapter 2, library media users should have high expectations in terms of the levels of curriculum support services and skills instruction provided. At the same time, users have the responsibility to support, in words and behavior, the efforts of library media professionals.

Cooperation and participation do not occur magically. Library media staff must work to gain the confidence and respect of users. Support then becomes an upward spiral: the library media program provides quality services, users are satisfied and support the library media program, the program expands and improves the services offered. Of course, the opposite can occur as well: lack of support leading to poor program development, leading to even less support. A positive attitude along with communication and public relations can go a long way to seeing that reality is the former.

As with the program feasibility analysis, the final result of the resources feasibility stage is a priority listing of curriculum units (with associated curriculum support services and library & information skills). Thus, by the end of stage 4, feasibility has been determined from two perspectives: program and resources. The first and primary focus is on services and instruction, however the priority listing is also based on realistic expectations given anticipated levels of available resources.

With priorities established and a listing of appropriate units in hand, planning, stage 5, becomes a manageable activity.

CHAPTER 7

The Six-Stage Strategy:

Review Situation | Goals and Objectives | Support Systems | Feasibility Analysis | Develop Plans | Evaluate Plans

Stage 5: Develop plans

Stage 6: Evaluate plans and processes

This chapter completes the explanation of the Six-Stage Strategy. **Developing plans**, stage 5, includes both comprehensive and operational planning. Overall, comprehensive planning provides direction and a framework for program development over a five year period. Specific unit and lesson plans offer operational guidelines for implementation of the library & information skills instruction. Stage 6 involves the **evaluation** of (1) plans, (2) the program, and (3) the effectiveness of the overall Six-Stage Strategy.

• • •

STAGE 5: DEVELOP PLANS

There is a natural flow from feasibility analysis (stage 4) to planning (stage 5). The decisions reached in the feasibility stage are reflected in the priority listing of units. This listing is actually the first draft of a planning document. In the planning stage, the activities related to integrated library & information skills instruction and curriculum support services are further defined and articulated in relation to classroom curriculum units. On the comprehensive or macro level, plans are expressed within a rolling five-year and detailed one-year context. On the micro or operational level, expectations are articulated as unit plans and lesson plans.

Perhaps the easiest way to consider the planning stage is to explain the tools or instruments particularly useful for developing plans. Three levels of plans are offered here: (1) a rolling five-year plan, (2) detailed one-year plan, and (3) unit and lesson plans.

1. ROLLING FIVE-YEAR PLAN

As explained in chapter 3, a rolling five-year plan begins with the detailed plan for year 1 and projects four more years into the future. Plans for each succeeding year are less specific. The plan is "rolling" because at the end of year 1, projection is again made five years into the future. The original year 2 becomes year 1 and so on.

A rolling five-year approach is recommended for planning on a number of levels. For example, beyond the curriculum-related functions of the library media program, a comprehensive five-year plan is suggested for guiding the entire library media program. Starting with the overall goals of the program, the plan outlines the acquisition, allocation, and use of resources to solve identified problems and meet stated objectives. In each succeeding year, the level of specificity decreases, that is, objectives, problems, and actions are stated in less and less detail.

As noted previously, overall planning for the library media program is beyond the scope of this book. However, a five-year planning approach applies to the development of curriculum-related plans as well. From a curriculum concerns perspective, a rolling five-year plan can be developed that focuses on support services, the library & information skills curriculum, and identified curriculum units.

Figure 7.1. Structure for Five-Year Plan

	YEAR 1	YEAR 2	YEAR 3	YEAR 4	YEAR 5
Goal:					
Objectives:					
Associated Problems/ Needs:					
Components of the problem:					
Actions:					
Criteria for Evaluating Success:					

Figure 7.2. Alternate structure for a five-year plan

YEAR:

GOAL:

RELATED OBJECTIVE

ASSOCIATED ASPECTS

ACTIONS: library media

ACTIONS: others

TIME FRAME:

EVALUATION:

The five-year plan must be based on *realistic expectations* in meeting stated goals and objectives. The goals and objectives were defined in stage 2, and realistic expectations were determined in the feasibility analysis, stage 4. The task in stage 5 is to outline a specific plan for the next year and increasingly general plans for the following four. Figure 7.1 is a suggested format for a five-year plan.

The purpose of the five-year plan is to lay out, in broad terms, the objectives, activities, and time schedule for meeting the major goals associated with curriculum support services and library & information skills instruction. In figure 7.1, curriculum goals are identified and described in terms of objectives, problems/needs, aspects of those problems/needs, actions, and criteria for evaluation. For each of these categories, statements of intent and involvement are noted *by year*. It is not expected that each category will have information for each year. On the contrary, there should be blank spaces throughout the overall plan. This shows, in graphic terms, how different aspects of the program are to be developed at different times.

The actual tasks or activities to be carried out are noted in the *Actions* category. While this is obviously a key category, it is important that tasks and activities be considered within the context of meeting objectives and solving identified problems.

There are, of course, many possible ways of presenting this material. One alternative is to organize the plan by year (see figure 7.2). Each year is a broad heading and related categories are listed under each. Library media specialists are encouraged to choose or design a planning structure that best fits their own purposes. Looking at existing planning documents in the school district is also recommended.

2. Detailed One-Year Plan

One-year plans provide more detail on meeting goals and objectives. The overall one-year plan should be structured in the same way as the five-year plan. That is, the categories remain the same, however much more specific information needs to be included on problems and actions. In addition, the one-year plan needs to lay out in more specific terms: (1) the sequence and time frame of targeted units, (2) related library & information skills, and (3) relevant curriculum support services.

Three tools are useful for presenting additional one-year information:

1. a schedule of selected curriculum units;
2. a skills-by-unit matrix;
3. a support services-by-unit matrix.

1. Schedule of curriculum units

The schedule of curriculum units is a chronological chart of those units selected as appropriate for integration with library & information skills instruction and/or in need of curriculum support services. Units to be included are selected from the priority listing developed in the feasibility stage.

The schedule is based on a technique of systems analysis used for project management called a *Gantt chart*. A Gantt chart is a time line that outlines those activities or tasks necessary to complete a project. From a Gantt chart, it is easy to determine when tasks begin and end, which tasks rely on each other or must be completed before others can begin, and the overall flow of a project. For planning curriculum-related activities of the library media program, there are similar concerns.

For example, while there is usually some way of noting unit name, teacher, grade, and subject on the schedule of curriculum units, the most useful information relates to *time frame* and *sequence*. From the schedule, it should be possible to ascertain when units begin, the duration of units, and when they end. Even a quick glance should indicate periods of heavy or light demand on the library media program. More in-depth study should reveal overlap, conflicts, as well as units with potential for interdisciplinary cooperation.

Figure 7.3a is a partial schedule for a K - 6 elementary school.* The units

---

* Figures 7.3a and 7.3b (and all other figures in this chapter) are based on the same elementary and secondary school situations as the curriculum maps in chapter 8. The figures are intended as examples and do not include comprehensive information for each situation.

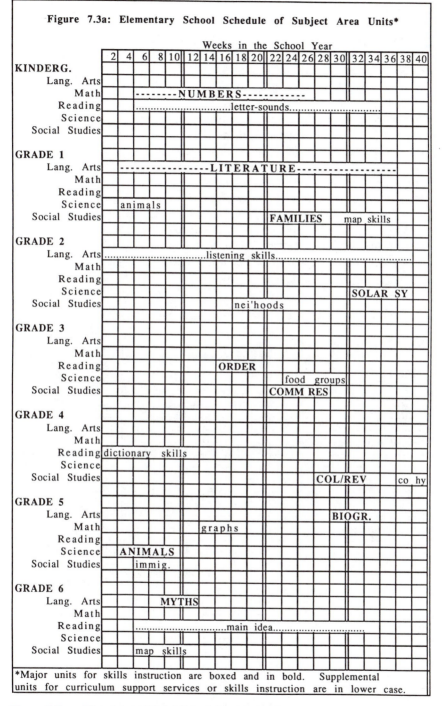

Figure 7.3a: Elementary School Schedule of Subject Area Units*

Weeks in the School Year

| | 2 | 4 | 6 | 8 | 10 | 12 | 14 | 16 | 18 | 20 | 22 | 24 | 26 | 28 | 30 | 32 | 34 | 36 | 38 | 40 |

KINDERG.
Lang. Arts
Math ....NUMBERS...........
Reading ....letter-sounds..........................
Science
Social Studies

GRADE 1
Lang. Arts ....LITERATURE..................
Math
Reading
Science animals
Social Studies FAMILIES map skills

GRADE 2
Lang. Arts ....listening skills..........................
Math
Reading
Science SOLAR SY
Social Studies nei'hoods

GRADE 3
Lang. Arts
Math
Reading ORDER
Science food groups
Social Studies COMM RES

GRADE 4
Lang. Arts
Math
Reading dictionary skills
Science
Social Studies COL/REV co hy

GRADE 5
Lang. Arts BIOGR.
Math graphs
Reading
Science ANIMALS
Social Studies immig.

GRADE 6
Lang. Arts MYTHS
Math
Reading ....main idea..........................
Science
Social Studies map skills

*Major units for skills instruction are boxed and in bold. Supplemental units for curriculum support services or skills instruction are in lower case.

**Figure 7.3a. Elementary School Schedule of Subject Area Units
The Six Stage Strategy: Stages 5 and 6**

designated for major integration with library & information skills instruction are noted in bold and capital letters. Additional units requiring curriculum support services or useful to supplement skills instruction are noted in lower case. Analyzing the schedule, it seems that skills instruction is reasonably spread over the year and across the major subject areas. The year begins primarily with major efforts in grades 5 and 6. During the middle of the year the focus is on K through 4. Grades 1, 3 and 5 are more than adequately covered with two major units each while 2, 4, and 6 have only one major unit and may require more attention. Grade 2 in particular, is not scheduled for a major skills instruction unit until the last quarter. This situation should be corrected.

Figure 7.3b represents a 10-12 secondary school and offers a slightly different format. Here only the major units are listed, and some units are listed more than once. Courses in high school may only last 10 or 20 weeks and then repeat for different student groups. In these situations, it is appropriate to list the units more than once on the schedule to reflect when units are taught during the year.

Figure 7.3b: Secondary School Schedule of Selected Subject Area Units

Gr	Subject	Weeks in the School Year																				
		2	4	6	8	10	12	14	16	18	20	22	24	26	28	30	32	34	36	38	40
1 0	Art		Waterc										Waterc								
1 0	Biology																		Genetics		
1 0	Biology												Human Body								
1 0	English 2						Short Story										Short Story				
1 0	Health			Drugs					Drugs					Drugs					Drugs		
1 0	Math 2	Lin. Eq.																			
1 0	World Hy.		Gr. Myth.																		
1 1	Amer. Hy.	Early Imm.																			
1 1	Amer. Hy.												Twenties								
1 1	Business I								Advertis.										Advertis.		
1 1	Chemistry			Mo. Bond.																	
1 1	English 3											Shakespeare									
1 1	French 3		Fr.cook.										Fr.cook.								
1 1	Physical Ed.																Tennis				
1 2	AP Biology											Indep. Study									
1 2	English 4	Persuas. Speech										Persuas. Speech									
1 2	Govern't																	Cold War			
1 2	Govern't						Sup. Ct.														
1 2	Indust. Arts	Robotics											Robotics								
1 2	Physics													Music							
1 2	Spanish																		Travel		

Figure 7.3b.   Secondary School Schedule of Selected Subject Area Units

Although the schedule represents only a portion of the overall curriculum, it does appear that the second quarter (encompassing weeks 11–20) is particularly light. Perhaps additional units can be identified (from the overall curriculum map) for special development in this time period. It may also be a good time for scheduling special events or tackling time-consuming administrative tasks.

The schedule of curriculum units is intended to be a planning tool and should be used as such. This means that the information should not be taken as final in any way. If necessary, units can be dropped from consideration or altered, or others added. Even this brief analysis of figures 7.3a and 7.3b reveals that adjustments in both the elementary and secondary plans are necessary and appropriate.

In reviewing the schedule and developing a plan, it will likely be desirable to consult with teachers and administrators. It may also be useful to refer back to the curriculum maps and to the priority listing from the feasibility analysis.

Ultimately, the schedule of units should stand as a planning document outlining the chronological schedule of classroom curriculum units to be integrated with library & information skills instruction or to receive curriculum support services. It may be useful to indicate whether the units listed on the schedule are targeted for library & information skills instruction and/or curriculum support services. This can be done by color-coding, using some other means for differentiating between units, or by having two separate schedules.

After a rough draft of the schedule is in place, it is important to take a closer look at the skills and services associated with particular units. The skills-by-unit matrix and support services-by-unit matrix are tools designed for these purposes. Note that the information revealed in the matrices may also indicate that changes need to be made in the overall plan.

2. Skills-by-unit matrix

The skills-by-unit matrix is intended to provide detail on the relationship between library & information skills and selected classroom curriculum units. A matrix is a chart with rows and columns. The rows represent one dimension, the columns another. In the skills-by-unit matrices (figures 7.4a and 7.4b), the curriculum units are listed as rows (on the left side of the chart) and the Big Six Skills are listed as columns (across the top). The organization of units in the matrix depends upon how classes and subjects are organized in the school.

For example, for the school represented in figure 7.4a (the same elementary school situation as figure 7.3a), the grade, calendar quarter, subject, and unit name are noted. The units are listed in order by grade and calendar quarter. For the secondary school matrix (figure 7.4b), it is enough to note the grade, subject, and name of the unit. A place for brief comments is available in both charts. It may be important to include the teacher's name to differentiate among teachers doing the same unit in the same grade but with significantly different approaches.

More detailed information on a particular unit is always available from the curriculum maps or from talking with teachers. Also, if the overall amount of information is too great to easily view in one chart, separate matrices can be developed for each grade level, calendar quarter or subject area.

A dot (•) in the matrix indicates the intersection of a unit and a particular skill. While it is recommended that the general information problem-solving process (the Big Six Skills) be reviewed and reinforced with every unit, certain units will be targeted for more detailed skills development. A skills-by-unit matrix notes the specific skills to be stressed with particular units.

Figure 7.4a: Elementary School Skills by Unit Matrix (sorted by grade and calendar quarter)										
GR	CQ	Subject	Unit	THE BIG SIX SKILLS						Comments
				1	2	3	4	5	6	
0	1111	Reading	Letter-Sounds			•				year long
0	1110	Math	Numbers	•	•		•			use in LMC
0	0010	Social Studies	Families							
0	0001	Science	Plants/Seeds							
1	1111	Language Arts	Literature	•		•		•		major unit
1	1000	Science	Food Groups							
1	1000	Science	Animals	•	•					stress strategy
1	0011	Social Studies	Map Skills				•	•		use and present
1	0010	Social Studies	Families-World	•				•	•	eval = product
1	0010	Art	Clay							
2	1111	Language Arts	Listening Skills		•		•			audio tapes
2	1111	Language Arts	Grammar							
2	0110	Social Studies	Neighborhoods					•		project
2	0100	Music	Rhythm							
2	0001	Science	Solar System	•		•	•			multi sources
2	0001	Social Studies	Goods & Services							
3	1111	Language Arts	Grammar							
3	0111	Math	Multiplication							
3	0100	Reading	Order of Events					•	•	generalize
3	0100	Language Arts	Fables/Poetry							
3	0010	Science	Food Groups				•			
3	0010	Social Studies	Comm. Resources	•	•	•		•		maj. create guide
4	1100	Reading	Dictionary Skills			•	•			
4	1000	Science	Work and Energy							
4	0110	Social Studies	Colonial/Revolut.	•	•				•	small tasks
4	0100	Language Arts	Letter writing							
4	0010	Art	Paper Mache							
4	0001	Social Studies	County History			•		•		
5	1000	Science	Class. of Animals	•				•	•	taxonomy
5	1000	Social Studies	Immigration		•	•				
5	0100	Math	Graphs/Charts				•			
5	0011	Language Arts	Biography		•			•	•	special unit
5	0010	Art	Printmaking							
5	0001	Social Studies	Nation's Growth							
6	1111	Language Arts	Critical Writing	•		•				stress task & loc
6	1111	Reading	Main Idea				•			
6	1100	Language Arts	Mythology		•			•	•	major unit
6	1100	Social Studies	Map Skills				•	•		expand skills
6	1000	Science	Hearing/Sound							test
6	0010	Science	Electricity							

Figure 7.4a.　Elementary School Skills by Unit Matrix

Gr	Subject	Unit	1	2	3	4	5	6	COMMENTS
		Figure 7.4b: Secondary School Skills by Unit Matrix (sorted by grade and subject)							
			THE BIG SIX SKILLS						

Figure 7.4b: Secondary School Skills by Unit Matrix
(sorted by grade and subject)

Gr	Subject	Unit	THE BIG SIX SKILLS 1	2	3	4	5	6	COMMENTS
10	Art	Watercolors							
10	Biology	Genetics	•				•		computer sim.
10	Biology	Human Body	•	•	•	•	•	•	major unit
10	English 2	Short Story					•	•	write story
10	Health	Drugs	•	•			•		"say no" brochure
10	Math 2	Linear Equations							
10	World History	Greek Mythology				•	•		interdisc.
11	American History	The Twenties			•		•	•	high potential
11	American History	Early Immigrants	•	•					test
11	Business 1	Advertising							
11	Chemistry	Molecular Bonding							
11	English 3	Shakespeare							
11	French 3	French Cooking				•	•	•	sources & product
11	Physical Ed.	Tennis							
12	AP Biology	Independent Study	•	•	•	•	•	•	Big Six bonanza
12	English 4	Persuasive Speech	•	•	•	•	•	•	major unit
12	Government	Cold War							
12	Government	Supreme Court Cases				•	•	•	important for skills
12	Industrial Arts	Robotics	•			•	•		demo product
12	Physics	Physics of Music		•	•				hard to find
12	Spanish	Travel				•	•	•	eval. info. sources

Figure 7.4b. Secondary School Skills by Unit Matrix

From figure 7.4a, a number of important facts are easily ascertained about the elementary school program. For example, the grade 2 science unit *solar system* requires information gathered from more than books, therefore location & access and use of sources are stressed; the *biography* unit in grade 5 and the *mythology* unit in grade 6 both emphasize the more difficult skills of synthesis and evaluation; the grade 2 *listening skills* unit stresses strategies to find needed resources and the use of those resources (here audio cassette tapes); and in grade 3, the *community resources* unit focuses on synthesis as the assignment calls for compilation of a community resources file. Even in kindergarten, there are opportunities for Big Six Skills instruction as students are taught how to look at number books (an information use skill).

Similar information is available from the secondary school skills-by-unit matrix (figure 7.4b): the 10th grade health unit *drugs* culminates in student-created brochures (a synthesis activity); task definition and information seeking strategies are part of the *immigration* unit in grade 11 American history while a later unit, *the twenties*, focuses on location & access, synthesis and evaluaton; task definition and information seeking strategies are also stressed in the grade 12 *physics of music* unit.

In addition to looking at individual units, a skills-by-unit matrix can be analyzed (1) to insure that each grade adequately covers the full range of skills, (2) to see that skills instruction is integrated across subject areas, and (3) to document the anticipated breadth and emphasis in skills instruction.

From both matrices (figures 7.4a and 7.4b), it is clear that more than one skill is associated with each unit, and that, in most grades, each of the Big Six Skills receives adequate attention. Furthermore, in the elementary school, skills instruction appears reasonably spread-out across subjects and units. The secondary school matrix shows a different pattern. Here, skills instruction is more concentrated in major units for grades 10 and 12 (*human body* and *persuasive speech* respectively) while little instruction is carried out in grade 11 beyond the American history curriculum. While recognizing that the examples here do not include data on the full curriculum, figure 7.4b may be an indication that more thought needs to be given to the 11th grade situation.

As with the schedule, adjustments in the one-year plan may be necessary based upon review of the matrix. If a particular skill area is not stressed, it may be wise to add a unit or change the skills emphasis for an existing unit. Similarly, if a skill area is receiving too much attention, units may be dropped or revised. The skills-by-unit matrix provides information for planning purposes as well as documentation of planning decisions.

3. Support services-by-unit matrix

Similar in design to the skills-by-unit matrix, the support services-by-unit matrix provides detail on specific curriculum support services activities and related subject area units (see figures 7.5a and 7.5b). Again, the rows in the matrix represent classroom curriculum units. The columns now represent curriculum support services (for example, materials provision, media production services, instructional design, reading guidance). The particular curriculum support services listed should reflect those offered by that particular library media program as listed in the curriculum support services checklist. For ease of viewing, it is recommended that the names of services be abbreviated or coded. For figures 7.5a and 7.5b, the major curriculum support services are:

    rp - resources provision,
    rg - reading guidance,
    is - information service,
    cc - curriculum consultation, and
    cd - curriculum development.

The support services-by-unit matrix reveals the nature and scope of curriculum support services related to specific units. It also indicates the level of support planned for different subjects, grades, and/or teachers. As with the schedule and skills-by-unit matix, the matrix will likely lead to adjustments in the one-year plan.

A wide range of curriculum support services are anticipated for the K -6 elementary school represented in figure 7.5a. Overall, the heaviest service de-

Figure 7.5a: Elementary School Support Services by Unit Matrix
(sorted by grade and calendar quarter)

GR	Subject	Unit	CURR. SUPPORT SER					Comments
			rp	rg	is	cc	cd	
0	Reading	Letter-Sounds	•	•				year long/ multiple materials
0	Math	Numbers	•	•			•	stories
0	Social Studies	Families						
0	Science	Plants/Seeds						
1	Language Arts	Literature	•		•		•	major unit/need prep time
1	Science	Food Groups	•					
1	Science	Animals	•	•				booktalk
1	Social Studies	Map Skills			•	•		materials for class
1	Social Studies	Families-World	•	•	•		•	major skills unit
1	Art	Clay						
2	Language Arts	Listening Skills	•	•		•		stations - tapes
2	Language Arts	Grammar						
2	Social Studies	Neighborhoods	•			•		project
2	Music	Rhythm						
2	Science	Solar System	•			•	•	major skills unit/multi mats.
2	Social Studies	Goods & Services						
3	Language Arts	Grammar						
3	Math	Multiplication						
3	Reading	Order of Events	•	•			•	booktalk
3	Language Arts	Fables/Poetry	•					materials to class
3	Science	Food Groups	•					
3	Social Studies	Comm. Resources	•		•	•	•	create resource guide
4	Reading	Dictionary Skills				•	•	work with teacher
4	Science	Work and Energy						
4	Social Studies	Colonial/Revolut.	•	•		•	•	major support unit
4	Language Arts	Letter writing						
4	Art	Paper Mache						
4	Social Studies	County History	•		•			locally collected materials
5	Science	Class. of Animals	•		•	•	•	creative unit
5	Social Studies	Immigration	•					display in LMC
5	Math	Graphs/Charts	•					
5	Language Arts	Biography	•	•		•	•	special unit/LMC activities
5	Art	Printmaking						
5	Social Studies	Nation's Growth						
6	Language Arts	Critical Writing			•			
6	Reading	Main Idea	•	•				booktalk
6	Language Arts	Mythology	•	•	•	•	•	lots of services needed
6	Social Studies	Map Skills	•			•		different map sources
6	Science	Hearing/Sound						
6	Science	Electricity						

Figure 7.5a.   Elementary School Support Services by Unit Matrix

mand is for resources provision. This includes providing materials to be used in the library media center as well as compiling temporary collections to be sent to the classroom. Beyond providing resources, there are units that require direct information service. For example, for the *county history* unit in grade 4 the library media specialist gathers information about local history and makes it available through a variety of formats including a fact sheet, a database on historical sites, and a resource file of brochures, pamphlets and memorabilia.

By definition, those major units targeted for integration with library & information skills instruction require curriculum development services. These are

Figure 7.5b: Secondary School Curriculum Support Services by Unit Matrix
(sorted by grade and subject)

Gr	Subject	Unit	CURR. SUPP. SERV.					COMMENTS
			rp	rg	is	cc	cd	
1 0	Art	Watercolors						
1 0	Biology	Genetics	•			•		computer sim.
1 0	Biology	Human Body	•		•	•	•	major unit
1 0	English 2	Short Story	•	•		•		booktalk
1 0	Health	Drugs	•			•		brochure
1 0	Math 2	Linear Equations						
1 0	World History	Greek Mythology		•	•			interdisciplinary/booktalk
1 1	American History	The Twenties	•		•	•	•	major unit
1 1	American History	Early Immigrants	•			•		potential - work w. teachers
1 1	Business 1	Advertising						
1 1	Chemistry	Molecular Bonding						
1 1	English 3	Shakespeare						should be involved
1 1	French 3	French Cooking	•		•	•		fun unit/ see skills
1 1	Physical Ed.	Tennis	•					impt. to fulfill needs
1 2	AP Biology	Independent Study				•	•	see skills/ impt. for AP kids
1 2	English 4	Persuasive Speech	•			•	•	media resources/major unit
1 2	Government	Cold War						
1 2	Government	Sup. Court Cases	•		•	•	•	requires major support
1 2	Industrial Arts	Robotics	•		•	•		
1 2	Physics	Physics of Music	•			•		hard to find mats.
1 2	Spanish	Travel		•		•		booktalk

Figure 7.5b.   Secondary School Curriculum Support Services by Unit Matrix

joint efforts between library media specialists and teachers. In figure 7.5a, those units targeted for curriculum development are those receiving significant attention in the skills-by-unit matrix (figure 7.4a). Curriculum consultation is less formal interaction regarding the use of library media center resources or services with particular aspects of instruction. The matrix also indicates that there is at least one reading guidance service intended for each grade. In most instances this will be accomplished through a booktalk, display, resource list, or bibliography.

The secondary matrix (figure 7.5b) provides similar information. It too closely relates to the skills-by-unit matrix (7.4b) as those units important for integration with skills instruction (e.g., *human body, the twenties, French cooking, persuasive speech*, and *Supreme Court cases*) often require major curriculum support services. In this particular secondary school example, there is less demand for reading guidance and more for curriculum consultation. Consultation is especially important in secondary schools as teachers may be unaware of how library media center services and materials can be used effectively to meet the needs of highly structured (and often mandated) curriculum units.

The support services-by-unit matrix is an easy to create and highly useful tool for displaying and documenting planned curriculum support activities with associated units. When used in combination with the schedule and the skills-by-subject matrix, the library media specialist has detailed information as well as an overall picture of the curriculum-related aspects of the library media program.

OTHER FORMS OF PRESENTING ONE-YEAR PLANS

There are alternative ways to document and present the one-year plans. Figure 7.6, for example, is a chart combining the chronological sequence of units with associated library & information skills (the Big Six Skills) and curriculum sup-

Figure 7.6: Elementary School Year Schedule: Includes Big Six Skills, Curriculum Support Services, and Comments

Subject	Weeks in the School Year (content)	Big Six Skills to emphasize (1 2 3 4 5 6)	Comments
KINDERG.			
Lang. Arts			
Math	--NUMBERS [rp rg cd]------	1 2 4	major unit
Reading	...................letter-sounds........[rp rg cd].........	3	year long
Science			
Soc Studies			
GRADE 1			
Lang. Arts	----------------LITERATURE---[rp rg cd]------	1 3 5	major unit
Math			
Reading			
Science	animals [rp rg]	1 2	btalk
Soc Studies	FAMILIES map skills [rp gp is cc] [is cc]	1 4 5 6	major unit
GRADE 2			
Lang. Arts	...........listening skills.[rp rg cc]............	2 4	audio tapes
Math			
Reading			
Science	SOLAR SY [rp cc cd]	1 3 4	major unit
Soc Studies	nei'hoods [rp cc]	5	
GRADE 3			
Lang. Arts			
Math			
Reading	ORDER [rp rg cd]	5 6	
Science	food groups [rp]		
Soc Studies	COMM RES [rp is cc cd]	1 2 3 5	great unit
GRADE 4			grade needs wk.
Lang. Arts			
Math			
Reading	dictionary skills [cc cd]		1st unit
Science		5 6	
Soc Studies	COL/REV co hy [rp rg cc cd] [rp is]	1 2 3 5 6	major unit
GRADE 5			good year
Lang. Arts	BIOGR.	2 5 6	major unit
Math	graphs [rp is cc cd] [rp rg cc cd]	4	
Reading			
Science	ANIMALS [rp]	1 5 6	expand grl
Soc Studies	immig. [rp]	2 3	
GRADE 6			
Lang. Arts	MYTHS [rp rg is cc cd]	2 5 6	major unit
Math			
Reading	...........main idea.......[rp rg]...........	4	
Science	elec. [cc]		
Soc Studies	map skills [rp cc]	4 5	

*Major units for skills instruction are boxed and in bold. Units for curriculum support services or involved in supplemental instruction are in lower case.

Figure 7.6. Elementary School Year Schedule: includes Big Six Skills, curriculum support services, and comments

port services. While it may appear desirable to combine all relevant data in one place, it is recommended that plans not be overly cluttered. Too much detail on one chart can hinder the ability to review and analyze the plans, and thus overlook potential problem areas.

Planning information can also be stored and presented via a computer database. Reports generated from the database can provide the kind of information presented in the chronological schedule and matrices. It is possible either to create a database structure from scratch or to extend the database already developed for curriculum mapping.

To adapt the curriculum mapping database:

(a)   select those curriculum units identified as particularly appropriate for library & information skills instruction or requiring curriculum support services.
(b)   store these units, with all fields, in a separate database.
(c)   Add the following fields to the new database:

- LIBRARY & INFORMATION SKILLS
- CURRICULUM SUPPORT SERVICES
- LIBRARY & INFORMATION TEACHING TIME: direct teaching time by the library media specialists
- LIBRARY & INFORMATION SKILLS TIME: scheduled time in the library media center.

With this information available in the database, a number of different reports can be created to present and document plans, schedules, and the scope of activities.

The schedule, matrices, and computer database are all tools designed to articulate and present the detailed one-year plan. They are more specific than the overall, five-year plan, but are still not on the operational level. Operational planning is done through unit and lesson plans.

UNIT AND LESSON PLANS

Unit and lesson plans outline the curriculum at its most fundamental level. Unit plans state the objectives, topics, sequence, teaching methods, materials, organization, and evaluation of curriculum units. In the library media context, unit plans must articulate both the subject area *and* library media components. Lesson plans provide details on the content and the specific learning activities of daily instruction.

There are many formats for unit and lesson design. Frameworks for designing unit and lesson plans integrating library & information skills and subject area content are presented and explained in chapter 11. Also included are examples of integrated units and lessons.

$$\bullet \quad \bullet \quad \bullet$$

The planning processes and tools described above represent the culmination of the four stages prior to planning. Plans provide an agenda; they state in a five-year, one-year, or daily context what the curriculum-related activities of the library media program should be. They do not guarantee success. As English called curriculum guides "fictional" so too are plans fictional. It remains for creative, building-level library media specialists to turn plans into reality.

STAGE 6: EVALUATE PLANS AND PROCESSES

The overall purpose of this final stage of the Six-Stage Strategy is to determine whether stated goals and objectives are met. There are three major aspects to stage 6: (1) the evaluation of the plans, (2) the evaluation of the program, and (3) the evaluation of the strategy. Although evaluation is a continuing process and occurs throughout the strategy, it also must take place more formally. Plans must be evaluated before implementation to determine if they address the stated goals and objectives and have a reasonable chance of succeeding. After plans have been implemented, the curriculum-related aspects of the library media program must be evaluated in terms of original goals and objectives. Finally, the strategy itself must be evaluated to determine its usefulness in meeting program needs.

1. Evaluate plans

As noted, evaluation is a continual process throughout the Six-Stage Strategy. At each of the five preceding stages, reviewing situation, defining goals and objectives, setting up support systems, feasibility, and planning, there has been a review of conditions, a determination of needs, and decisions as to direction and actions. However, before implementation, there needs to be a systematic evaluation of plans. In general, do the plans reflect what is desired? Do they address stated goals and objectives?

More specifically, at each level of planning (five-year, one-year, unit and lesson), do the plans as developed meet the perceived needs? It is therefore appropriate to evaluate plans at each level.

Evaluation of the Five-Year Plan

The rolling five-year plan outlines goals and objectives, problems, and actions relating to overall library & information skills instruction and curriculum support services for a five-year period. Evaluation seeks to determine whether the plans adequately cover the curriculum-related goals and objectives as stated.

Questions to be asked include:

- Are the goals and objectives as outlined, obtainable in a five-year period?
- Will the actions have the desired result?
- Is it reasonable to expect the actions outlined to be carried out within five years?

The five-year plan is integrally tied to overall planning for the library media program. Evaluation of the five-year plan therefore must also include deciding whether the curriculum-related objectives and needs are adequately expressed in the general library media plans. In particular, are there plans for obtaining the necessary resources?

Evaluation of one-year plan

In the section on the one-year plan (above), four tools were used to describe one-year plans: the overall one-year plan (based on the five-year structure), the schedule of units, the skill-by-unit matrix, and the services-by -subject matrix. In evaluating these, collectively or separately, certain key questions need to be asked.

In general,

- Are the five-year goals and objectives reflected in the one-year plan?
- Is it reasonable to expect the actions listed to be carried out?
- If all actions are completed, will the objectives be met?
- Are there any glaring missing or weak spots in the one-year plan?

Regarding the library & information skills curriculum,

- Are the Big Six Skills adequately covered?
- Is there room for more detail?
- Is the plan attempting too much?
- Is the schedule reasonably spread out?
- Do units cover a range of subject areas?
- Is there appropriate instruction in each grade level?

Regarding curriculum support services,

- Have the needs of all teachers been identified?
- Are there plans to meet the basic support service needs of each teacher?
- Have the needs of administrators been considered?

- Is there planning for a range of support services?
- Is the plan attempting too much?
- Is the schedule reasonably spread out?
- Are there additional support services that should be considered in the future?

These questions (and others relating to individual needs) can aid in determining if the one-year plan addresses the needs as defined and if it is reasonable to expect that the plan will succeed. This evaluation will determine whether the plans should be implemented as is or if there is a need for major revision.

Evaluation of unit and lesson plans

Unit and lesson plans are plans at the operational level. They must be evaluated in terms of:

- Do they address stated objectives?
- Will they motivate students?
- Are the instructional variables adequately stated?
- Are required materials, facilities, equipment available?
- Is there a mechanism for evaluating student achievement?

Evaluation of units includes review by teachers. Ideally, teachers should be involved in planning from the beginning. Hopefully, the type of planning group recommended in the section on support systems is already in place. This local planning group can be particularly helpful in evaluating unit plans. In addition, teachers scheduled for cooperative, integrated units should have the opportunity to review and evaluate unit plans. Their reactions will be important for insuring successful implementation of units.

Lesson plans are more individual and specific than unit plans. While teacher input may be useful on the lesson level, generally, it is not necessary. Library media specialists will want to review lesson plans to insure consistency with unit objectives and recommended activities.

2. Evaluation of the program

The evaluation of plans explained above deals primarily with evaluation prior to implementation. Plans seek to spell out how objectives are to be met, not whether they have actually been met. Therefore, at some point after implementation, more general questions relating to the program must be asked and answered.

First, there needs to be a determination as to whether the plans have been followed.

- Again, have the stated objectives been met?

- Have activities, units and lessons been implemented successfully?
- What seemed to work particularly well?
- What areas were a problem?

Answering these and related questions will provide guidelines for future planning and lead to revision as necessary.

Beyond evaluating the implementation of plans, there also needs to be an evaluation of the existing state of curriculum-related functions. In effect, this is equivalent to stage 1 of the Six-Stage Strategy, review the existing situation. Thus there is both the completion of the strategy and a natural feedback to the beginning stage. As explained early on, the process is circular, with evaluation leading back to review, redefinition, and replanning.

3. Evaluation of the Six-Stage Strategy

Finally, there needs to be an evaluation of the Six-Stage Strategy itself.

- Did the strategy work in this particular school situation?
- Were there specific problems?
- Are there some procedures that were particularly useful?
- Are there areas that need more work?

Evaluating the Six-Stage Strategy is not a black-or-white, success-failure statement. Rather, evaluating the strategy should serve as a guide to future changes in approach and emphasis. The Six-Stage Strategy needs to be adapted to local concerns and mechanisms. Thus, the evaluation of the strategy is important to overall planning and program development.

• • •

This concludes the explanation of the Six-Stage Strategy. It has been stressed that not every task, activity, or tool needs to be implemented. The essence of the strategy is following a systematic approach. As noted in the introduction to Part II, the strategy is a cycle of information gathering, analysis, planning, and evaluation. Again, there will be adaptation to meet needs of individual situations. The overall theme is that successful integration of a library & information skills curriculum and meaningful curriculum support services requires a thought-out, systematic strategy.

PART III

CURRICULUM: INFORMATION AND FUNCTIONS

The curriculum concerns of the library media program center around the curriculum of the school, library & information skills instruction, and curriculum support services. While introduced in earlier chapters, Part III goes into more depth on concerns and approaches in each of these areas.

The objectives in Part III are to:

- use curriculum mapping for collecting, storing, retrieving, and presenting curriculum information,
- develop an expanded view of the curriculum support service role of the library media program,
- outline a critical thinking-based library & information skills curriculum,
- offer a structure for designing integrated unit and lesson plans,
- summarize and look to the future.

Curriculum mapping is a technique for gathering, storing, and displaying curriculum information. By evaluating curriculum maps, the library media specialist is able to determine (1) the need for curriculum support services and (2) those units in the curriculum most suitable for integration with library & information skills instruction. Chapter 8 explains curriculum mapping in detail.

The curriculum-related functions of the school library media program are two-fold: curriculum support services and library & information skills instruction. Curriculum support services are intended to meet the needs of classroom instruction and overall curriculum development. Chapter 9 examines a broad approach to curriculum support, one that goes well beyond the traditional role of materials provision.

Likewise, the approach to library & information skills instruction, outlined in chapter 10, is non-traditional. This is reflected in the term "library & information skills" as opposed to "library skills" or "library media skills." The skills curriculum outlined in chapter 10 is unique in a number of ways. First, it models the information problem-solving process. Second, it is top-down—starting broadly with the BIG SIX SKILLS and outlining all other skills within the BIG SIX SKILLS context. Last, the library & information skills curriculum is approached from a critical thinking skills perspective. This refers to the taxonomy of the cognitive domain developed by Benjamin Bloom (1956). In each of the BIG SIX SKILLS areas, the sequence of skills moves from a basic knowledge level up to evaluation.

Moving back from comprehensive concerns to the operational level, chapter 11 offers a structure for considering and designing unit and lesson plans. These plans integrate classroom content and library & information skills instruction. Examples of integrated units and lessons are included in the chapter.

Chapter 12 concludes Part III and the book. Its purpose is to tie things together as well as look ahead to developing trends in curriculum concerns.

CHAPTER 8

Curriculum Mapping: Collection, Organization and Evaluation of Curriculum Information

Underlying every aspect of the Six-Stage Strategy is the idea of bringing together the library media program with the curriculum of the school. The ultimate goal is to match the library media program with the curriculum content of the classroom. For this to occur, it is essential that up-to-date, accurate information on curriculum be readily available. Unfortunately, systematic curriculum information is rarely present.

This chapter outlines a technique for gathering and evaluating information about the curriculum in a given school: *curriculum mapping*. Originally developed by Fenwick English (1978, 1979, 1980), curriculum mapping is a method for collecting, storing, and reporting curriculum information. Eisenberg (1984) successfully adapted and expanded curriculum mapping for use in library media situations. The resulting curriculum maps provide the information required for relating library media curriculum support services and library & information skills instruction to the curriculum of the school. The objectives of this chapter are to:

- explain the need for curriculum information,
- describe the technique of curriculum mapping,
- outline the steps in curriculum mapping: data collection, storage, and presentation,
- investigate how to evaluate curriculum maps for library media purposes.

• • •

EXISTING SOURCES OF CURRICULUM INFORMATION

Curriculum information is the foundation for general planning in the school, as well as for library media program planning. The most common source of information for elementary and secondary education is the *curriculum guide*: state, district or building-level. These guides, often created by a committee of teachers and administrators, are intended to provide direction as to the content and conduct of classroom instruction. The most well-known of these are the global guides published by the education departments of all states for most subject areas. These guides provide a valuable overview of what the curriculum *should be*, what is considered important state-wide, and serve as a common point of reference for the various schools in a state. Although a general sequence of topics and time frame are usually noted, there is little attempt to specify the degree of emphasis or schedule of particular topics. For the library media program, these guides are of limited value in identifying key areas for integration or support, as they do not represent the actual classroom curriculum.

District or building-level guides are more detailed in outlining subject areas and sequences within and across grade levels. Fenwick W. English, referring to these local curriculum guides, acknowledges that "curriculum guides assist teachers in knowing that a topic or subject came before or will come after another topic in a particular K-12 sequence, but within these parameters, the amount of time, emphasis, pacing, and iteration are the domain of teachers to decide." (1980, p. 149) Even these local guides are of limited value for the library media specialist interested in analyzing existing curricula. The guides are vague, lack specificity, and do not represent the actual curriculum as applied by individual teachers.

English (1978) has also referred to curriculum guides as "fiction." Curriculum guides offer the "intended" curriculum, noting what some group would like the curriculum to be, what it should be, what it is hoped to be. Curriculum guides are not based on the reality of day-to-day instruction and do not provide library media specialists with the detailed, accurate information needed for planning support services and integrated skills instruction.

There are a number of sources that provide real, "nonfiction" information about the curriculum. The textbooks used, the unit and lesson plans of teachers, and the assignments given to students all reflect, to some degree, the curriculum as implemented in the classroom. From these sources, it may be possible to determine the approaches and topics in the curriculum, the expectations of teachers, as well as the emphasis, time, organization, and materials of instruction.

Unfortunately, the availability and reliability of these sources are limited. For example, not all teachers use textbooks, and those who do often skip large sections. Similarly, teachers differ as to detail in unit and lesson plans and may be reluctant to share full plans and assignments. Finally, even if the library media specialist were to undertake the major task of systematically gathering these materials, the necessary organization, analysis, evaluation, and summary efforts would be overwhelming.

This is not to suggest that access to these kinds of sources would not be valuable. Library media specialists are encouraged to collect curriculum guides, texbooks, unit and lesson plans, and particularly assignments. Still, there is a clear need for a systematic and relatively efficient means of gathering, storing, presenting and reviewing curriculum information.

CURRICULUM MAPPING

Library media specialists need accurate assessments of the current state of affairs in a school. A process for identifying the status quo, for revealing the existing curriculum has been labeled *curriculum mapping* by Fenwick English. A curriculum map is a "descriptive portrait of what tasks [were undertaken] and how much time [was] spent on any given set of items, concepts, skills or attitudes. A map is not a lesson plan. A map is past oriented; it is a recording of what was taught." (English, 1979) Mapping is intended to reveal the bottom line, the actual curriculum being taught to students.

English bases curriculum mapping on the descriptive research method of content analysis. Content analysis relies on analyzing written or oral communications by such procedures as counting the number of newspaper pages or column inches dedicated to various issues in order to determine predominant attitudes, interests or values. A curriculum map documents curriculum in much the same way. English (1978), for example, collected information of the time spent and level of instruction (introduced, reinforced or expanded) on various topics within a K-12 science curriculum to determine previously hidden priorities, overlap, and biases. Results could then be compared to stated objectives and used as the basis for restructuring, planning and resource allocation.

Eisenberg (1984) adapted and expanded curriculum mapping for use in school library media skills contexts. In addition to data on topics, time frame, and level of instruction, planning for school library media programs requires information about teaching methods, organization of students (groupings), the materials of instruction, and evaluation methods. While collecting information on these additional aspects poses no problem, the storage and display of information on many items is more difficult and unwieldly. However, these problems are easily overcome by using any simple file or database program (e.g., Appleworks, dBASE, Reflex) on any personal computer (e.g., Apple, IBM, Macintosh). The remainder of this chapter outlines the mechanics of curriculum mapping in three steps: data collection, storage, and presentation. Evaluation of curriculum maps to identify units for curriculum support services or integration with library & information skills instruction is also discussed.

DATA COLLECTION

Gathering data for curriculum mapping is a relatively simple process:

(1) Establish the basic component of analysis. The fundamental organizational block for curriculum and instruction is the *unit*. Most subject areas and courses of study in elementary and secondary schools are designed as a series of units. Units are flexible—they may span two weeks or ten; include nine assignments or one. It is therefore appropriate to collect curriculum mapping information about curriculum units.

Figure 8.1:

Elements/Fields of Interest for Curriculum Maps

Unit	Level of Instruction
Grade	Teaching Methods
Subject	Resources/Materials
Total Periods	Grouping of students
of Instruction	Evaluation
Calendar Quarter	Teacher

Figure 8.1.   Elements/Fields of Interest for Curriculum Maps

(2) Identify the elements or *fields* of interest relating to units. Figure 8.1 outlines the fields of information about units that are particularly interesting for library media programming.

Minimally, school planning requires a knowledge of unit sequence and total time allotted for units in each grade level. In addition, for skills integration and support services, it is important to have information available regarding instructional methods, level, evaluation, organization, and resources. Fields of interest should be adapted to local needs. For example, it has been suggested that the numbers of different classes or numbers of students taught the unit be included as an additional field.

(3) Determine the type of data to be collected. Because curriculum mapping is past-oriented, it records what *exists,* not what *is intended.* Information compiled on what has taken place provides a solid base for planning. Certainly, adjustments will need to be made to accommodate changes from year to year. Logically, these adjustments take place during the feasibility or planning stages. For curriculum mapping, the focus must be on accurate, current information.

It is also important to be aware that it is not necessary to collect data on every unit. While the ultimate goal is to document as much of the curriculum as possible, an initial identification and gathering of information on a limited number of major units for each teacher or subject/grade level will provide an adequate, useful base for planning.

(4) Collect the actual data. There is no single, correct way to approach this step. English (1979) notes that using independent observers was a more reliable approach than requesting teachers to provide their own information. Unfortunately, that is not a very practical suggestion for most school situations.

More commonly, the library media specialist will initiate and coordinate the mapping procedure, collect data, and compile the maps. Figure 8.2 is a form designed for collecting mapping information and can be used in a number of

Figure 8.2:   Curriculum Mapping Worksheet

Date_____

Grade:_____ Instructor_____ Subject_____

Unit_____

Total Periods of Instruction_____

Calendar Quarter_____

Level of Instruction_____
    introduced
    reinforced
    expanded

Primary Teaching Method_____

desk work	programmed
lecture	(includes learning stations)
demonstration	project
discussion	report
independent study	combination

Materials:_____
    text
    one source
    multiple sources

Organization of Instruction_____

large group	individual
small group	combination

Evaluation_____

test	report
product	combination
observation	

Comments_____

Figure 8.2.   Curriculum Mapping Worksheet

different ways. Some library media specialists have found faculty meetings a useful place to introduce the mapping procedure and have each teacher fill out a form for one or two significant units. This can be followed up with additional forms and a request to teachers to document additional substantial units completed to date It may be sufficient to simply send forms to teachers with a cover note. Or it may be deemed worthwhile (and/or necessary) to sit down and work with teachers individually. At worst, the library media specialist may have to complete the mapping forms and request confirmation and/or changes from teachers.

It is crucial to gain the support of teachers and administrators for the mapping effort. Teachers need to be shown how the information supplied will result in better library media support for their classes and how easy it is to supply mapping information. Similarly, if the usefulness of mapping for administrative and educational development purposes can be demonstrated to administrators, they should enthusiastically support and assist in the effort.

All of these methods are reasonable approaches to data collection. In general, while some mapping efforts have met with resistance, more often teachers are enthusiastic and pleased that someone is taking an interest in what they are doing. In almost all instances, once the use, value, and ease of participating are made known, teachers and administrators are more than willing to cooperate.

DATA STORAGE: BUILDING THE CURRICULUM DATABASE

Once the curriculum information is collected, it must be organized and stored in a usable manner. In computer terminology, the *database* must be designed and created. With a limited number of elements, the information can be organized manually. However, with the large number of fields of interest to the library media program, manual compilation of curriculum maps is not really easy. In the long run, it is much more simple, efficient and effective to implement curriculum mapping using a personal computer and a file or database management program.

There are file or database management programs available for every type of personal computer. They range from simple systems, for example Appleworks, to more complex packages, for example dBASE II or III or Reflex. Programs differ as to options for storage, retrieval, display, speed of operations, and the size of the database that can be accomodated. Any file or database management program can be used for curriculum mapping.

Regardless of the program used, the procedures for creating a curriculum mapping database using a personal computer are essentially the same:

1. define the database structure;
2. document the controlled vocabulary; then
3. enter the data.

Figure 8.3: Curriculum Map Database Definition
using dBase II or III (on IBM)

```
Enter name, type, length ...
Unit, c, 15
Grade, n, 2
Subject, c, 15
Instructor, c, 3
Periods, n, 2
CelQ, c, 4
Level, c, 5
Methods, c, 10
Resources, c, 5
Organization, c, 2
Evaluation, c, 10
.
```

Figure 8.3. Curriculum Map Database Definition Using dBase II or III (on IBM)

Defining the database usually consists of indicating the fields in the database, the field names, field length, and the nature of data to be entered (text, numbers, logical information, etc.). This process of defining the structure varies slightly from one computer program to another. Appleworks and Reflex prompt the user for field names. Alternatively, dBASE requires specifying the lengths of each field and type of data. Figures 8.3 - 8.5 are samples of database definition for different systems.

Using a controlled vocabulary is important for data entry purposes, sorting, and analysis. For example, is the subject area to be called *language arts* or *English?* Is the evaluation method a *report* or a *paper ?* Decisions of this kind must be made before data entry. Similarly, appropriate abbreviations must be established and documented. The curriculum mapping worksheet, figure 8.2 above, suggests some terms to be used for each field.

Once the structure and vocabulary are fixed, data entry is possible. As with database definintion, the mechanics of data entry vary from system to system. While a few items may require interpretation by a library media specialist, data entry is generally a clerical task.

Lack of computer experience or access to a computer should not be viewed as a reason for not conducting curriculum mapping. There may be a teacher or

Figure 8.4:   **Curriculum Map Database Definition**
using Appleworks (on Apple II)

File: CURMAP   INSERT NEW RECORDS   Escape: Review/Add/Change

Record 1 of 1
==
GR: -
SUBJ: -
INST: -
UNIT: -
TOTAL PER: -
CQ: -
LEVEL: -
PTM: -
MATERIALS: -
ORG: -
LEVEL: -
EVAL: -
SUBMITTED BY: -

Type entry or use ⊖ commands   489K Avail.

Figure 8.4.   Curriculum Map Database Definition Using Appleworks (on Apple II)

Figure 8.5:   **Curriculum Map Database Definition**
using Reflex (on Apple Macintosh)

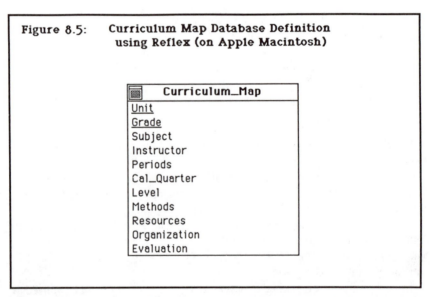

Figure 8.5.   Curriculum Map Database Definition Using Reflex (on Apple Macintosh)

78

administrator (or even a student!) in the school or district who can implement and manage the automated curriculum database. If computer-based mapping is truly not feasible, it is possible to create the curriculum database manually. The information can be stored in a file organized by grade or subject, and desired information can be pulled out as needed.

Figure 8.6: Elementary Curriculum Map
Full information sorted by grade/calendar quarter

Unit	Subject	Gr	Ins	Per	CQ	Level	Group	Mats.	Method	Eval.
Letter-Sounds	Reading	0	CMM	40	1111	intro	combinat	multiple	combinati	none
Numbers	Math	0	CMM	40	1110	intro	combinat	multiple	combinati	test
Families	Social Studies	0	CMM	5	0010	intro	large	none	combinati	none
Plants/Seeds	Science	0	CMM	4	0001	intro	large	none	combinati	none
Literature	Language Arts	1	WSE	120	1111	intro	combinat	multiple	combinati	combinat
Food Groups	Science	1	WSE	8	1000	intro	large	single	combinati	test
Animals	Science	1	WSE	15	1000	intro	combinat	multiple	combinati	test
Map Skills	Social Studies	1	WSE	35	0011	intro	combinat	multiple	combinati	project
Clay	Art	1	ACH	2	0010	intro	individu	none	desk work	product
Families-World	Social Studies	1	WSE	20	0010	intro	combinat	multiple	combinati	product
Listening Skills	Language Arts	2	BLB	180	1111	intro	combinat	multiple	combinati	combinat
Grammar	Language Arts	2	BLB	80	1111	intro	combinat	text	desk work	test
Neighborhoods	Social Studies	2	BLB	20	0110	intro	combinat	multiple	combinati	project
Rhythm	Music	2	BMC	10	0100	intro	large	multiple	lecture	test
Solar System	Science	2	BLB	15	0001	intro	combinat	multiple	combinati	product
Goods & Services	Social Studies	2	BLB	10	0001	intro	combinat	single	desk work	ditto
Grammar	Language Arts	3	FAC	80	1111	expa	combinat	text	desk work	test
Multiplication	Math	3	FAC	120	0111	intro	individu	text	desk work	test
Fables/Poetry	Language Arts	3	FAC	15	0100	reinf	combinat	multiple	large	none
Order of Events	Reading	3	FAC	20	0100	expa	combinat	multiple	combinati	ditto
Food Groups	Science	3	FAC	15	0010	expa	combinat	multiple	combinati	test
Community_Reso	Social Studies	3	FAC	10	0010	intro	small	multiple	combinati	project
Dictionary Skills	Reading	4	BDE	35	1100	reinf	individu	multiple	desk work	combinat
Work and Energy	Science	4	BDE	8	1000	intro	large	text	lecture	test
Colonial/Revolut	Social Studies	4	BDE	25	0110	intro	combinat	multiple	combinati	combinat
Letter writing	Language Arts	4	BDE	8	0100	intro	individu	single	combinati	product
Paper Mache	Art	4	ACH	8	0010	intro	individu	none	desk work	product
County History	Social Studies	4	BDE	15	0001	intro	large	multiple	lecture	test
Classif. of	Science	5	RAG	12	1000	expa	combinat	multiple	combinati	project
Immigration	Social Studies	5	RAG	5	1000	intro	small	multiple	combinati	ditto
Graphs/Charts	Math	5	RAG	10	0100	reinf	small	multiple	desk work	test
Biography	Language Arts	5	RAG	12	0011	expa	combinat	multiple	combinati	product
Printmaking	Art	5	ACH	7	0010	intro	combinat	multiple	desk work	product
Nation's Growth	Social Studies	5	RAG	8	0001	intro	combinat	text	combinati	test
Critical Writing	Language Arts	6	JMS	24	1111	expa	combinat	multiple	combinati	combinat
Main Idea	Reading	6	JMS	24	1111	expa	individu	multiple	combinati	combinat
Mythology	Language Arts	6	JMS	16	1100	expa	combinat	multiple	combinati	combinat
Map Skills	Social Studies	6	JMS	15	1100	expa	combinat	multiple	combinati	combinat
Hearing/Sound	Science	6	JMS	14	1000	intro	combinat	text	combinati	test
Electricity	Science	6	JMS	12	0010	intro	combinat	text	combinati	project

Figure 8.6. Elementary Curriculum Map (full information sorted by grade/calendar quarter)

DATA PRESENTATION: CURRICULUM MAPS

The collection and storage of curriculum information in a database is not a curriculum map. A *curriculum map* is a chart or table of curriculum information compiled from some or all of the elements in the curriculum database. Manually creating curriculum maps is a laborious and difficult task. This task is easily accomplished via computer as one of the major purposes of file or database management software (in addition to storing and organizing data) is to *display* information in some useful manner. This kind of printout is generally referred to as a *report*.

Page and type size limit what can be printed on a given page. It is generally not possible, nor desirable, to include all fields in each report. For ease of viewing and analysis, different reports consisting of certain fields are usually created. In addition, database management programs usually provide some

Figure 8.7: Elementary Curriculum Map
Resources = Multiple
Evaluation not test
Sorted by Subject

Subject	Gr	Unit	Resources	Evaluation
Art	5	Printmaking	multiple	product
Language Arts	1	Literature	multiple	combination
Language Arts	2	Listening Skills	multiple	combination
Language Arts	3	Fables/Poetry	multiple	none
Language Arts	5	Biography	multiple	product
Language Arts	6	Critical Writing	multiple	combination
Language Arts	6	Mythology	multiple	combination
Reading	0	Letter-Sounds	multiple	none
Reading	3	Order of Events	multiple	ditto
Reading	4	Dictionary Skills	multiple	combination
Reading	6	Main Idea	multiple	combination
Science	2	Solar System	multiple	product
Science	5	Classif. of Animals	multiple	project
Social Studies	1	Families-World	multiple	product
Social Studies	1	Map Skills	multiple	project
Social Studies	2	Neighborhoods	multiple	project
Social Studies	3	Community_Resources	multiple	project
Social Studies	4	Colonial/Revolution	multiple	combination
Social Studies	5	Immigration	multiple	ditto
Social Studies	6	Map Skills	multiple	combination

Figure 8.7. Elementary Curriculum Map (information sorted by subject, resources = multiple, evaluation not test)

Figure 8.8: Elementary Curriculum Map: K - 3
Focus on variables of instruction

Gr	Subject	Unit	Level	Methods	Res.	Organiz.	Evaluation
0	Math	Numbers	introd	combina	multip	combina	test
0	Reading	Letter-Sounds	introd	combina	multip	combina	none
0	Science	Plants/Seeds	introd	combina	none	large	none
0	Social Studies	Families	introd	combina	none	large	none
1	Art	Clay	introd	desk	none	individu	product
1	Language Arts	Literature	introd	combina	multip	combina	combina
1	Science	Animals	introd	combina	multip	combina	test
1	Science	Food Groups	introd	combina	single	large	test
1	Social Studies	Families-Worl	introd	combina	multip	combina	product
1	Social Studies	Map Skills	introd	combina	multip	combina	project
2	Language Arts	Grammar	introd	desk	text	combina	test
2	Language Arts	Listening	introd	combina	multip	combina	combina
2	Music	Rhythm	introd	lecture	multip	large	test
2	Science	Solar System	introd	combina	multip	combina	product
2	Social Studies	Goods &	introd	desk	single	combina	ditto
2	Social Studies	Neighborhood	introd	combina	multip	combina	project
3	Language Arts	Fables/Poetry	reinfor	large	multip	combina	none
3	Language Arts	Grammar	expand	desk	text	combina	test
3	Math	Multiplication	introd	desk	text	individu	test
3	Reading	Order of	expand	combina	multip	combina	ditto
3	Science	Food Groups	expand	combina	multip	combina	test
3	Social Studies	Community_R	introd	combina	multip	small	project

Figure 8.8.   Elementary Curriculum Map: K - 3 (focus on variables of instruction)

mechanism for selecting out and/or sorting certain parts of the database. It may be desirable to view only those units that take place in third grade or that use a report as the evaluation method. Most database programs can handle these requests easily.

Figure 8.6 - 8.10 are examples of presenting curriculum information in curriculum maps. The examples were created using the Reflex program on the Apple Macintosh personal computer. Figure 8.6 is a curriculum map with all fields included for a K–6 elementary school.* Figures 8.7 and 8.8 are alternative maps for the same setting. Figure 8.9 represents full information on units from a 10–12 secondary school. For figure 8.10 only those units spanning 10 or more periods are included.

---

* Both the elementary and secondary maps are based on the same situations as presented in chapter 7. Again, the figures are intended as examples and do not include comprehensive information for each situation. For example, only one teacher per grade level and selected units for those teachers are shown. Special thanks to Christine Lauster for assisting in compiling the elementary school information.

Figure 8.9: Secondary Curriculum Map
Full information sorted by grade/calendar quarter

Gr	Subject	CQrtr	Unit	Ins	Per	Level	Group	Mats.	Meth	Eval.
10	Health	1111	Drugs	CAE	10	expan	combinat	multip	combinat	product
10	Art	1010	Watercolors	VRT	10	expan	individu	none	lab	product
10	World History	1000	Greek	NSK	10	reinfo	combinat	multip	combinat	product
10	Math 2	1000	Linear	MAS	6	introd	large	text	desk	test
10	English 2	0101	Short Story	MPB	24	reinfo	large	multip	combinat	product
10	Biology	0010	Human Body	REB	50	expan	combinat	multip	combinat	combination
10	Biology	0001	Genetics	REB	10	expan	combinat	multip	combinat	product
11	French 3	1010	French cooking	JAC	6	introd	combinat	multip	lab	product
11	Chemistry	1000	Molecular	JBB	5	expan	large	text	lecture	test
11	American	1000	Early	TMJ	8	expan	combinat	multip	combinat	test
11	Business 1	0101	Advertising	APD	9	introd	large	text	lecture	test
11	English 3	0010	Shakespeare	LIE	15	expan	large	single	lec/dis	test
11	American	0010	The Twenties	TMJ	20	expan	combinat	multip	combinat	combination
11	Physical	0001	Tennis	CJI	9	introd	individu	single	lab	none
12	Industrial	1010	Robotics	AJB	20	introd	individu	multip	lab	product
12	English 4	0101	Persuasive	JAS	15	expan	combinat	multip	combinat	product/obs
12	Government	0100	Supreme Court	ASV	12	introd	combinat	multip	combinat	product
12	AP Biology	0010	Independent	PMS	20	expan	individu	multip	indep	product
12	Physics	0010	Physics of	DJS	8	introd	combinat	multip	combinat	paper
12	Government	0001	Cold War	ASV	6	introd	large	text	lec/dis	test
12	Spanish	0001	Travel	STL	8	expan	small	multip	combinat	product

Figure 8.9. Secondary Curriculum Map (full information sorted by grade/calendar quarter)

Figure 8.10: Secondary Curriculum Map: Grades 10 - 12
Major Units (10 or more periods)
Sorted by Periods and Grade

Unit	Subject	Grade	Pers	Resources	Quarter
Human Body	Biology	10	50	multiple	0010
Short Story	English 2	10	24	multiple	0101
The Twenties	American History	11	20	multiple	0010
Independent Study	AP Biology	12	20	multiple	0010
Robotics	Industrial Arts	12	20	multiple	1010
Shakespeare	English 3	11	15	single	0010
Persuasive Speech	English 4	12	15	multiple	0101
Supreme Court Cases	Government	12	12	multiple	0100
Watercolors	Art	10	10	none	1010
Genetics	Biology	10	10	multiple	0001
Drugs	Health	10	10	multiple	1111
Greek Mythology	World History	10	10	multiple	1000

Figure 8.10. Secondary Curriculum Map: Grades 10 - 12 (major units, 10 or more periods, sorted by periods and grades)

DATA EVALUATION: ANALYZING CURRICULUM MAPS

For the library media program, the ultimate purpose in creating curriculum maps is to determine those units most appropriate for integration with library & information skills instruction or in need of curriculum support services. As noted in chapter 6, this is the heart of program feasibility analysis.

Certain attributes should be considered when evaluating curriculum maps to determine units for integration with skills instruction. Particularly appropriate units usually:

- are of significant duration;
- are a major emphasis in the curriculum;
- use multiple, nontext sources;
- use methods other than lecture;
- are reinforced or expanded level;
- have a flexible organization of instruction; and/or
- use creative assignments or evaluation techniques other than test.

For curriculum support services also look for units that:

- use a combination of teaching methods;
- require multiple materials; and/or
- rely on a product, project, paper, or report for evaluation.

There is no single correct way to analyze curriculum maps. One approach is to narrow the search step-by-step by selecting units because they have certain attributes. For example, if the objective is to identify units for integration with library & information skills instruction, the first step might be to select those units that result in a report, project, product, or paper. Next see which of those units require multiple materials and a combination of teaching methods. Lastly, examine the remaining units by grade, subject, and instructor to insure that final selections span the necessary grades and cover a range of subject areas.

Based on these criteria, units from the sample maps (figures 8.6 - 8.10) that seem particularly appropriate for integration with library & information skills instruction can be identified.

On the elementary level these include:

unit	subject	grade
numbers	math	K
literature	language arts	1
families	social studies	1
solar system	science	2
order of events	reading	3

community resources	social studies	3
colonial/rev. period	social studies	4
biography	language arts	5
animals	science	5
mythology	language arts	6

On the secondary level these include:

unit	subject	grade
human body	biology	10
the twenties	American history	11
independent study	ap biology	12
persuasive speech	English 4	12
Supreme Court cases	government	12

Units that need curriculum support services can be identified in a similar fashion. The library media program should be involved in the development of major curriculum units, particularly those that will be used for integrated skills instruction. In addition, units that rely on multiple materials and require students to turn in a paper, report, product or project probably require curriculum support services. From the curriculum maps, it is easy to locate those units taking a relatively large number of periods and also requiring multiple materials and a report or project (see figures 8.7 and 8.10).

Identifying units can also be done through elimination. That is, there is little interest in those units primarily using a lecture teaching method, textbook, and having a test as the evaluation method. Units can be eliminated from consideration because they contain one or more of these attributes.

All these selections, searches, and sorts can be done through examining a general curriculum map or by using the capabilities of database management programs to refine the display. Most programs will allow selecting and sorting on designated criteria. Reports can then be generated based on these actions. These selected reports represent more limited curriculum maps and are highly useful for analysis and evaluation.

Finally, rather than select or eliminate units step-by-step, it may be valuable to consider the maps from a more global or *holistic* perspective. Here the most general curriculum map is reviewed and analyzed until something "jumps out." While this may be more time consuming and seem less systematic than a deductive approach, the results can be most revealing—particularly for identifying units with potential for interdisciplinary cooperation. Sometimes just looking at a map for a while will inspire insights or new relationships.

CHAPTER SUMMARY

Recognizing the importance of accurate, up-to-date curriculum information to the Six-Stage Strategy, this chapter has outlined the technique of curriculum mapping. Curriculum mapping can provide the information base necesssary to coordinate successfully a library media curriculum support services and skills program with the everyday activities of the classroom. Computer file or data management systems provide an efficient and flexible way of storing and retrieving curriculum information. Computer-based mapping allows the library media specialist to view and analyze the information in a variety of ways. With information on the school's curriculum in hand, the library media specialist is in a position to consider appropriate support services and library & information skills. Curriculum support services are considered in chapter 9, the skills curriculum in chapter 10.

CHAPTER 9

Curriculum Support Services Concerns of School Library Media Programs

This chapter gives an overview of the five curriculum support services roles and their associated activities: (1) curriculum resources support, (2) reading guidance, (3) information service, (4) curriculum consultation, and (5) curriculum development. In addition to instruction in library & information skills, the library media program has a major role in curriculum design, development, implementation, and evaluation. Through an understanding of these curriculum support services roles, library media specialists can become more involved in the full range of the curriculum processes within their school and district. The objectives of this chapter are to:

- present the expanded view of the curriculum support service roles of the library media program;
- examine activities, functions, and services within each role;
- understand the interrelated nature of curriculum support services roles;
- explain the potential offered by these roles.

• • •

As stated in Chapter 1, curriculum translates instructional goals into action. In so doing, curriculum determines the basis for the relationships between people (students, teachers, library media specialists), and content (what is taught and how it is taught). This relationship is symbiotic in that one element cannot properly function without the other, and both benefit. Like any other such system, the people-curriculum relationship requires support to be viable. In today's information-rich environment, the library media specialist has a multifaceted role to play in curriculum support.

Curriculum support has been a traditional role of library media specialists. Most often, this has involved providing resources to teachers, classrooms or to students. Typically this support is aimed at meeting needs associated with assignments, the last aspect of curriculum. In this book, we champion a new perspective for curriculum support services, one that challenges the status quo and requires a higher degree of responsibility and competence. Here, curriculum support services takes on a new meaning, with widened parameters. This role assumes full participation in the creation and initiation of curriculum.

What follows is a redefinition of the phrase *curriculum support services,* one that incorporates five interrrelated areas of concern: *(1) resources provision, (2) reading guidance, (3) information service, (4) curriculum consultation,* and *(5) curriculum development.* In individual situations, library media specialists fulfill these roles with varying degrees of involvement and influence. However, every library media specialist has fundamental responsibilities in each of these five areas.

To be optimally effective, the five curriculum support service roles must be understood in terms of who does what and why. It is important that library media specialists understand and be able to carry out the support service alternatives within each of the major support service roles. Therefore, library media specialists must be aware of curriculum goals, objectives, content, and methods. In order to gain credibility with teachers and administrators, library media specialists must possess competencies in teaching and instructional design, as well as information service and materials provision. Additionally, library media specialists must be skilled in human relations, able to interact with school administrators, teachers, and students to attain goals and objectives.

Therefore, in providing a full range of curriculum support services, library media specialists must be able to draw on knowledge and abilities inherent to:

- social foundations of education
- curriculum theory
- curriculum development process
- teaching-learning theory
- instructional materials design
- information service
- information resources management
- human relations
- marketing and public relations.

It is the combination of competencies in these areas that are important in order to bring reality to the potential curriculum service roles and translate theory into action.

1. RESOURCES PROVISION

Traditionally, library media programs have demonstrated their value to the educational program through the provision of space, materials and equipment to meet content curriculum needs (Liesener, 1976). This *resources provision* role has been described as support for, extension of, and complementary to the goals of the content area curriculum. Teachers and administrators readily accept this most essential, traditional curriculum support services role for library media specialists.

The resources provision role gives the library media program credibility and an initial involvement in curriculum. Paradoxically, at the same time, this role can severely limit broader influence and involvement for the library media program in the school's curriculum program. Too often, resources provision is a passive, reactive activity. Teachers design and implement curriculum; the library media specialist struggles to provide necessary resources after the fact. Even partial success in meeting resource needs under these circumstances reinforces the passive, reactor relationship of the library media program to curriculum. Library media specialists can become involved *before* implementation and assume a more active and effective role in resources provision by knowing the curriculum in advance (by reviewing curriculum maps, for example), and by working with teachers.

Resources provision centers around school library media specialists' competencies in accessing and organizing materials, equipment, and facilities. Library media specialists assess information needs, build resource collections, and design appropriate services and programs. The responsibility is to serve the predetermined purposes of the content curriculum. The library media specialist who is successful at resources provision develops an atmosphere that encourages teachers and students to avail themselves of library resources and services. This reinforces the use of non-textbook sources of information to teach content curriculum.

While the preceding explains resources provision in traditional terms (that is, selection, acquisition, organization and circulation of collections), the curriculum resources provision role is extended by (1) use of audiovisual and computer technologies, (2) networking with other library media centers and systems, (3) use of community resources, and (4) online information services. Effective curriculum resources support also overlaps with the other curriculum support service areas of reading guidance, information service, consultation, and curriculum development.

The full range of curriculum resources provision is limited only by the collective imaginations of school library media specialists. Figure 9.1 is a checklist of the types of services offered by school library media specialists in resources provision.

These services are not on the periphery of the educational program. They are basic, bottom-line requirements for the successful implementation of subject area curriculum. Through active provision of curriculum-related resources, the library media program meets the needs of the school curriculum. Futhermore, this approach establishes credibility for more extensive involvement in curriculum. Therefore, the challenge in the resources provision role is to provide appropriate and timely resources support, not as a reaction to classroom events, but jointly

Figure 9.1.   Resources Provision Services Checklist

The library media specialist:

☐ organizes materials for quick and easy storage, access, retrieval, and use;

☐ selects and acquires new curriculum-related resources;

☐ provides access to a full range of information resources and collections;

☐ provides access to audiovisual equipment for production and viewing;

☐ provides access to information resources beyond the school library media center through interlibrary loan and networks;

☐ uses online database services to find sources of information for students, teachers and administrators;

☐ provides guidance in materials selection to student and teachers;

☐ develops flexible scheduling;

☐ develops reserve materials collections;

☐ informs teachers of new resources available in the library media center;

☐ instructs students and faculty in the use of av equipment and software;

☐ builds a collection of current information about instructional materials and equipment;

☐ provides access to state curriculum manuals, district curriculum guides;

☐ provides a collection of professional educational materials; and

☐ hosts special co-curricular events in the library media center.

planned by teachers and library media specialists during the curriculum decision-making process. Resources provision lays the foundation for all other curriculum support service activities.

2. READING GUIDANCE

While closely related to resources provision, the services associated with reading guidance deserve special attention. Promotion of literacy and guidance in reading are long-standing concerns of all types of libraries. Traditionally, a major portion of the efforts of library media specialists have involved literature and reading. This involvement typically starts with selection, acquisition and organization of a collection of appropriate fiction and nonfiction materials. Library media specialists begin to offer guidance in reading and the selection of literature through such methods as bibliographies and displays. These services can be considered as curriculum support services when tied to classroom requirements or activities. Examples of typical reading are:

- showing the biography section to fourth grade students who are required to read about famous persons and give short presentations to the class;
- creating a bibliography of nineteenth centry American literature for tenth grade students required to read pre-twentieth century authors;
- sending a collection of alphabet books to the first grade classroom.

As with materials provision, reading guidance can be passive or active. In a passive mode, the library media program offers a range of reading guidance services but waits for teachers or students to initiate contact. A more aggressive approach is to anticipate needs and reach out to the classroom with appropriate services and activities. Active involvement from a reading guidance perspective includes working with teachers to (1) select reading materials for use in the classroom, (2) develop classroom activities and assignments that rely on outside reading, and (3) integrate special promotional activities (e.g. reading contests, Parents as Reading Partners, authors in the schools) with classroom curriculum.

Booktalks are a particularly useful, active service for reading guidance (Eisenberg & Notowitz, 1979). Booktalks have multiple objectives: to provide materials that meet the students needs, to excite students about books, and to involve the library media program in the curriculum activities of the classroom. A booktalk can be effective whenever a class has an assignment that involves selection of reading materials. While it is true that booktalks are valuable activities at any time, the booktalk is particularly effective and well-received by students and teachers when tied to an assignment.

For a curriculum-related booktalk, the library media specialist and teacher should jointly determine the nature of the assignment, needs of students, and purpose of the booktalk. The library media specialist then selects a group of books that meet the requirements as determined. From this group, a subset is selected for presentation to the class (the rest can be put on display in the library media center). In the actual booktalk, each book is discussed *briefly*, and not always with a summary of the plot. Comments on the author, subject area, genre, or how the book meets the needs of the assignment may be sufficient to motivate students to want to read the book. Thus, it is *not* necessary to be intimately familiar with each book. However initial selection of the book for inclusion should be based on careful evaluation.

Used in this fashion, the booktalk becomes a highly effective technique for promoting literature, guiding students in reading, and bringing the library media center into the curriculum. After booktalks have become an established part of the reading guidance program, displays, classroom collections, and bibliogra-

---

Figure 9.2: Reading Guidance Services Checklist

The library media specialist:

☐ provides an extensive collection of reading materials, fiction and nonfiction;

☐ provides bibliographies or pathfinders on reading materials related to specific needs: assignments, grades, subjects, reading levels;

☐ provides recreational reading lists;

☐ creates displays in the library media center;

☐ provides nonbook media related to literature;

☐ provides individual guidance to teachers, students, and administrators in the selection of reading materials;

☐ offers booktalks in the library media center or classroom;

☐ provides special events and activities to promote reading.

---

phies become even more effective as students and teachers become aware of the expertise of the library media specialist and the value of the advice offered.

Figure 9.2 outlines selected reading guidance services. Some of the items could be listed under one or more of the other support services areas; however reading guidance is a unique and important function and services associated with reading guidance warrant special note. The list is by no means comprehensive. As with all the checklists presented in this chapter, individuals are encouraged to expand on the selections and develop their own unique support services.

Reading guidance should make use of the full range of media to encourage reading and interest students in books. Library media specialists have a full complement of options (including slide/tape shows, films, videotapes, and computer programs) that can be used to help students to understand the plots, characters and major themes in literature.

When effectively used and integrated with other active curriculum support services, reading guidance becomes an essential component of the library media program.

3. INFORMATION SERVICE

Information service is an area closely related to other curriculum support services, particularly resources provision. It is considered separately here in order to emphasize that there is a difference between directing someone to an information source and actually giving someone direct information. In practice, information service can be considered as a spectrum, ranging from directing a person to a source, to assisting someone in locating and retrieving the source, to teaching someone how to locate and use information, and finally to providing direct answers. Figure 9.3 is a checklist of information service support activities.

Library media specialists are also information specialists. They are experts in the information problem-solving process, know how to find information, and can directly answer questions. While instruction in library & information skills is a major responsibility of the library media specialist, there are also times when it is more appropriate to directly provide a source of information or the information itself.

Consider, for example, an assignment in the secondary social studies curriculum that requires students to analyze decisions of the U.S. Supreme Court. Students are to choose a case, summarize the issues, report the decision, and discuss the long and short-term effects of the decision. This assignment clearly calls for locating and using nontext materials, but in this situation, the major instructional objectives are not oriented to having students themselves locate the information. In fact, requiring students to locate the resources on their own may actually get in the way of classroom objectives. Therefore, in this situation, the library media specialist has a responsibility to help select, locate and provide appropriate materials to the classroom or place them on reserve in the library media center. In addition, students needing more information should feel comfortable in requesting direct information service from the library media specialist.

The issue of how far the library media program should go in providing direct information service is a controversial one. Certain situations seem to call for direct information service, while others do not. In given curriculum situations, the need for information to meet subject area objectives must be coordinated and

---

Figure 9.3: Information Services Checklist

The library media specialist:

- [ ] creates a community resource file;
- [ ] provides curriculum information through curriculum maps;
- [ ] provides direct information service to students, teachers, and administrators;
- [ ] provides access to the ERIC database;
- [ ] uses ERIC to answer questions;
- [ ] uses other online information services to answer questions; and
- [ ] uses the telephone to answer questions.

balanced with objectives of the library & information skills curriculum. While it may be worthwhile to develop integrated units in certain instances, others are more appropriately handled through information service.

Creating and maintaining special information files or databases can also be considered as providing direct information service. Examples of these special files include:

- a community resource file of information about talented people in the community who might be available for school activities;
- a curriculum map providing information on what is going on in the school;
- the organizational structure support system: a file providing details on how the school and district are organized.

All these sources should be available for use by teachers and administrators. However, it is just as likely that the library media specialist will be asked questions about resource people (is there a local banker willing to speak to an economics class?), the curriculum (is anyone doing a unit on China during the spring semester?), or organization of the school (do all seventh-grade students take woodworking?) that call for direct answers. In these cases, the library media specialist will turn to the resources and provide direct information service.

Time, resources, support, and facilities can limit the extent to which library media specialists are able to provide direct information service. Still, in those situations deemed appropriate for direct information service, every attempt should be made to meet the needs of students, teachers, and administrators.

4. CURRICULUM CONSULTATION

A consultant is someone whose expertise is sought by others who need advice. The client typically has a high regard for the consultant's professional ability. Likewise, the consultant has high self-esteem. The overall perception is that the consultant knows about and does what others can merely guess at. Whereas the professional literature on library media specialists highlights changes in perception, the same literature substantiates the fact that library media specialists do not meet the definition of "consultant." In part, this is because library media specialists spend the majority of their non-instructional time and energies in a resources provision role, a role that is expected by everyone including the library media specialist. The result is that library media specialists have a minimal role as curriculum consultants yet have tremendous responsibility for providing the resources necessary for transforming the ideals for educating students into students who are ideally educated.

The library media specialist, acting in both formal and informal capacities, participates in the implementation of curriculum to improve the quality of curriculum and instruction. For example, curriculum maps created by library media specialists can provide specific information and an important perspective to teachers or administrators about the range and sequence of the school curriculum. Additionally, as a consultant to students, library media specialists can interpret curriculum for students attempting to complete library-related homework assignments.

Although the curriculum consultant role is often defined by and limited to predetermined curriculum needs that were discussed, decided, and developed without input from the library media specialist, this need not be so. Recently, more and more library media specialists are seen as assets to the implementation of units of study and individual lessons. Library media specialists are sought out for inclusion on building- and district-level curriculum councils as skilled advisors for curriculum implementation. This change from non-involvement to active participation in curriculum consultation redefines the role of the library media specialist within the curriculum decision-making process. Figure 9.4 is a list of curriculum consultation activities.

The decisions as to what will be taught, how it will be taught, and how it will be evaluated become day-to-day concerns and are legitimate components of the

Figure 9.4.   Curriculum Consultation Services Checklist

The library media specialist:

- [ ] interprets the information task within assignments for students;
- [ ] reviews appropriate library & information skills with teachers;
- [ ] maintains a library of professional educational resources;
- [ ] participates as a member of teaching teams;
- [ ] participates on school curriculum development committees;
- [ ] maintains a collection of educational resources catalogs;
- [ ] recommends informational resources for accomplishing unit and lesson objectives;
- [ ] informs teachers and administrators of new state or local curriculum guides and mandates;
- [ ] guides students and teachers in the selection of appropriate resources;
- [ ] evaluates curriculum from a library & information use skills perspective;
- [ ] supervises teachers and students in the use of instructional media;
- [ ] evaluates curriculum;
- [ ] prepares reviews on current education trends;
- [ ] brainstorms ideas for class projects;
- [ ] provides topics for research projects;
- [ ] serves on curriculum committees; and
- [ ] assists teachers in the development of instructional materials.

overall curriculum support services role. Acting in this way, library media specialists are active members of the instructional team. In addition, by being involved in curriculum decision-making, the library media specialist is in a better position to fulfill other support services and instructional roles.

5. CURRICULUM DEVELOPMENT

In many ways, curriculum development represents the highest level of curriculum support services and is the culmination of all other curriculum support activities. Curriculum development is dependent on professional competency and approach to instructional assessment techniques, design, implementation procedures, and evaluation methods. The development of curriculum involves a knowledge of learning theory, methodology, materials, and monitoring. Curriculum development also involves having the conviction to change the status quo through planning, politicking when necessary, and a commitment to a purpose.

To a large degree, these skills rest on training beyond the traditional library services training received in professional degree-granting programs of study. However, with the move from a passive to a more active role, programs of study are changing, and working library media specialists are seeking out opportunities for professional growth and retraining to gain these competencies.

Beyond resources provider and curriculum consultant, library media specialists can move to a position directly involved with planning, developing, implementing, and evaluating curriculum. The integrated library & information skills curriculum developed jointly by library media specialists and classroom teachers highlights (1) the interrelationship between library & information skills and subject areas and (2) the curriculum design and development skills of library media specialists. Curriculum development is a vitally important role because it guides practice and policy. The library media program has a central role in curriculum design development and the accomplishment of curriculum goals and objectives for all subject areas.

While the library media program has its own instructional goals and objectives, library media services are important to all content areas. As subject area curriculum becomes more and more information-dependent, and information problem-solving becomes a major concern throughout the instructional program, the role of the library media program becomes crucial. Ultimately, the library media center evolves into the focus and core of the school curriculum.

This has implications for the amount and kind of resources that are available to the library media center, and the degree of support the library center receives. As the curriculum role of the library media program expands, there is a new commitment to and ownership of the library media center by the school community.

This curriculum development role provides for the creation of new curriculum programs, units and lessons integrated with content area curriculum. As curriculum developers, library media specialists are in a position to aid the entire school program through highlighting the importance of (1) information, (2) information resources, (3) technology, and (4) the information problem-solving process to subject area curriculum. When successful in the curriculum development role, the library media specialist incorporates the other curriculum support services roles of resources provision, reading guidance, information service, and consultation.

In curriculum development, the library media specialist is as comfortable initiating curriculum programs as being responsive to others creating the curriculum. This role carries the highest responsibility as it encompasses the full range of curriculum activity, from assessment of need to evaluation of the implemented project. Curriculum development includes the articulation of purpose, goals, objectives, clearly stated learning outcomes and sound, research-based approaches to achieving those goals. Curriculum development involves the ability to be a visionary, to determine student needs along a lifelong spectrum of learning situations and information needs situations. Figure 9.5 outlines activities associated with curriculum development.

Figure 9.5. Curriculum Development Services Checklist

The library media specialist:

☐ focuses attention on instructional design process;
☐ creates programs where information skills bridge the gap between content areas;
☐ cooperates with teachers to design and implement units of instruction and daily lesson plans;
☐ develops curriculum to meet the requirement of the library & information skills scope and sequence;
☐ initiates and cooperatively writes integrated instructional units to meet students information skills needs;
☐ establishes guidelines for library & information skills instruction within the library media center and in the classroom;
☐ designs instructional systems;
☐ links people and nonprint resources through new methods of instruction;
☐ supervises the design of instructional materials; and
☐ evaluates the curriculum units and lessons developed for integrated library & information skills instruction

An active role in curriculum development changes the working relationship between the library media specialist, teacher and student, and at the same time changes the perception of the traditional role of the library media specialist. By taking advantage of this role, the library media specialist has the opportunity to move from supporting, extending or complementing classroom-based instructional programs to involvement and leadership in curriculum decision-making.

Again, the relationships that are developed in executing the responsibilities associated with curriculum design and development result in more than just successful educational programs and experiences for students. Library media specialists skilled in curriculum design and development increase their value by being able to participate and directly influence the creation of the curriculum from inception/conception to implementation of specific daily lesson plans. Curriculum that is coordinated, jointly developed, valued, sponsored, implemented and evaluated attests to the centrality of the library media program in the achievement of school-wide instructional goals and objectives.

It is possible for library media specialists to fulfill each of the interrelated curriculum roles. Sophistication in performing curriculum support services roles, as outlined, is central to the achievement of educational goals. Library media specialists have a unique vantage point to be able to see curriculum issues and set directions for resolving curriculum concerns. In so doing, it is possible for the library media specialist to move from a tangential to an integral curriculum position, from support to program ownership, from outside the curriculum process to strategic influence within the curriculum process.

The future direction of the curriculum services roles is determined by two factors: attititude and need. Attitude refers to the willingness of library media specialists to assume more extensive support services while integrating these with more traditional services. Need refers to the changing information needs of students and educators. It is the need to adapt to an information-oriented future— to think about, and plan for that future—that will most extend the curriculum support roles of the library media program. And, as options open for library media specialists and curriculum services roles expand, the library media center will act more as a center for the achievement of overall school goals.

CHAPTER 10

Library and Information Skills Curriculum Scope and Sequence: The Big Six Skills

The objectives of the library media program, from an instructional perspective, are articulated through a library & information skills curriculum (often referred to as a scope and sequence). A library & information skills curriculum sets the direction for the teaching/learning process, and provides a framework for clarity and continuity of instructional purpose. This chapter offers *The Big Six Skills*: a library & information skills curriculum designed around (1) the information problem-solving process and (2) Bloom's taxonomy of cognitive objectives. The emphasis is on developing a logical, critical-thinking approach to information problem-solving and not on those skills associated with merely locating and accessing information sources.

• • •

In this world of ever-increasing amounts of information, skills associated with information-seeking, use and communication are increasingly important. Library media specialists are educators who deal with information on a daily basis. They have the training and expertise to teach students the life-long skills needed to become *information literate*. To obtain this goal it is important to provide instructional opportunities for students to process, synthesize and evaluate information.

The library & information skills curriculum presented in this book, the *Big Six Skills*, is different than the traditional K-12 scope and sequence of library skills. First, it is based on the fundamental premise that there is a simple, logical approach to information problem-solving. This information problem-solving approach is adaptable to any information situation and is comprised of much more than just location and access to information.

Second, the *Big Six Skills* approach was designed within the context of Bloom's taxonomy of cognitive objectives (Bloom, 1956). Bloom describes a hierarchical classification of cognitive behavioral objectives. This widely-recognized, standard classification system for describing cognitive processes provides the foundation for a systematic approach to library & information skills instruction. The levels of cognitive behavior (knowledge, comprehension, application, analysis, synthesis, and evaluation) represent increasingly sophisticated levels of critical thinking. For the library media program, Bloom's classification holds the basis for developing skills objectives that encourage students to think by teaching students to think. Therefore, under each of the Big Six Skills, there are hierarchical skills objectives reflecting the levels of Bloom's taxonomy.

The key to effectively using the library & information skills curriculum presented in this chapter is understanding both the information problem-solving process and Bloom's taxonomy. Before presenting the full scope and sequence, more detail is given on each.

THE INFORMATION PROBLEM-SOLVING PROCESS

One of the major differences between the *Big Six Skills* curriculum and other library & information skills curricula is the emphasis on developing broad skills areas reflecting the information problem-solving process rather than teaching how to use specific resources, tools, or library systems. At some point, it may be desirable to teach the use of the *Readers' Guide*, but this instruction must be placed in the overall context of the information problem-solving process. This insures that skills instruction is fully integrated with classroom content and focuses on real information needs.

Information problem-solving is viewed as a systematic process consistent with the more general models of problem-solving presented in chapter 3. In this book, the information problem-solving process is presented as a series of six steps: the *Big Six Skills* (see figure 10.1). It is our contention that this general model can be used in all information problem-solving situations. Therefore, *whenever students are faced with information-related problems*, they should immediately think in terms of the *Big Six Skills*. That is, for meeting information needs, they should first apply the overall problem-solving model and later consider the specific requirements under each step.

The Big Six Skills curriculum is designed to promote and reinforce this top-down, problem-solving approach. Students should first develop an appreciation for the usefulness and applicability of the Big Six Skills approach to information problem-solving situations. Second, they should develop the specific skills necessary to carry out each of the six steps. Lastly, they should be able to evaluate their success in using the Big Six Skills to solve information problems.

In addition to making intuitive sense, *The Big Six Skills* approach is consistent with research findings regarding students and the research process. Based on a study of high school seniors, Carol Kuhlthau (1985a, 1985b, 1985c) developed a model of the library research process model closely related to the the Big Six Skills approach to information problem-solving. Kuhlthau found that "students not only needed but wanted guidance in the process which they were working

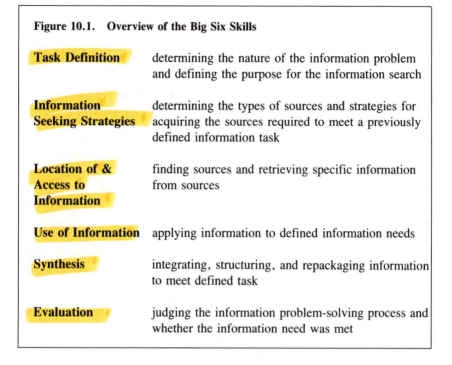

Figure 10.1.   Overview of the Big Six Skills

Task Definition   determining the nature of the information problem and defining the purpose for the information search

Information Seeking Strategies   determining the types of sources and strategies for acquiring the sources required to meet a previously defined information task

Location of & Access to Information   finding sources and retrieving specific information from sources

Use of Information   applying information to defined information needs

Synthesis   integrating, structuring, and repackaging information to meet defined task

Evaluation   judging the information problem-solving process and whether the information need was met

through as they were using the library." (1985a p. 35) She reports that by developing an understanding of the library research process, students are able to visualize what they will encounter and thus become more effective in using library resources. Most interestingly, Kuhlthau found that the students employ the same approach to research long after instruction in the process has ended.

BLOOM'S TAXONOMY OF EDUCATIONAL OBJECTIVES IN THE COGNITIVE DOMAIN

The second major influence on the design of the Big Six Skills is Benjamin Bloom's taxonomy of educational objectives in the cognitive domain (Bloom, 1956). This is a recognized system for describing and analysing the thinking process. While there are a number of alternative approaches to cognition (Piaget, 1952; Ennis, 1962), Bloom's taxonomy is used here because it (1) is widely known and accepted by educational professionals, and (2) provides a useful theoretical base for developing library & information skills objectives that challenge students to strive toward higher levels of thinking.

Bloom describes six levels of cognition (see figure 10.2). At each level, students can be expected to perform certain behaviors. Bloom defines the knowledge level as recall or recognition of ideas or facts usually in the same form in which it was taught. Repeating memorized content is an example of knowledge-level behavior. The comprehension level is the stage at which students' performance is characterized not only by understanding, but also by interpretating and extrapolating. Students can see, or propose relationships among ideas or facts as well as put content into their own words. At the application level students demonstrate the ability to use information for problem solving, applying ideas to new situations. Using content to solve new problems characterizes application-level behavior.

At the higher order level of analysis, students discover an idea's characteristics by breaking down an idea into its parts and discovering relationships. Analyzing content to find causes, conclusions, or supporting evidence is indicative of the analysis level. Synthesis is the level at which students create new ideas or patterns through divergent thinking. Synthesis involves rearranging content in new or original ways. Evaluation is the highest level of cognitive behavior. Here, students make critical judgments based on a preestablished set of criteria. Judging an idea's worth to the intended purpose is an evaluation-level behavior. Figure 10.2 matches Bloom's six levels of cognition to information-related behaviors.

The success of any curriculum concerned with critical thinking skills depends on having appropriate expectations for students. This requires asking the right questions at each level of Bloom's taxonomy. Examples of the type of questions associated with each level are noted in figure 10.3. In addition to questions, there are certain behaviors associated with each level. Appropriate vocabulary for

---

Figure 10.2. **Bloom's cognitive levels and associated information oriented actions**

☐ **Knowledge:** the ability to repeat appropriate information (with or without comprehension);

☐ **Comprehension:** the ability to demonstrate the understanding of information (e.g., translate/interpret/extrapolate);

☐ **Application:** the ability to transform information to find solutions to problems;

☐ **Analysis:** the ability to break information down into its parts/discover unique characteristics;

☐ **Synthesis:** the ability to combine information in order to uncover and develop relationships (e.g., hypothesize);

☐ **Evaluation:** the ability to make appraisals/judgments about information based on either external or internal standards.

Figure 10.3.   Questions linked to Bloom's cognitive levels (Berkowitz and Berkowitz, 1987)

☐ **Knowledge:**
Who, What, When, Where, How, Which questions.

☐ **Comprehension:**
Tell in your own words . . .
What can you infer about . . . why?
What do you predict will happen . . .?
What was the reason (cause/effect) . . .?

☐ **Application:**
How would he act in this new situation . . .?
If you were in the situation . . .?

☐ **Analysis:**
What is the main idea . . .?
What word appropriately describes . . .?
Find evidence that indicates that . . .

☐ **Synthesis:**
Using information from the article, rewrite the conclusion . . .
Tell a new story using the same characters . . .
Create a different solution for the same circumstances . . .

☐ **Evaluation:**
Which solution do you think is better? Why?
If you were in his situation, what would you have done?

---

writing behaviors linked to the different cognitive levels are given in figure 10.4. These words constitute the *active thinking vocabulary*.

Coordinating library & information skills with Bloom's cognitive theory results in a curriculum aimed at guiding students beyond knowledge and comprehension levels to the higher thinking skills levels of analysis, synthesis and evaluation. It is the ability to think at higher levels that allows students to attain transferable skills. When a student consciously recognizes that a skill mastered in one situation can be used in another situation, that student has a transferable skill. Examples of transferable skills include the ability to:

• define problems clearly;
• ascertain purpose
• organize through summarizing, outlining and notetaking;
• discern point of view;
• distinguish fact from opinion, bias and prejudice ;

Figure 10.4.   The active thinking vocabulary (Berkowitz and Berkowitz, 1987)

knowledge	comprehension	application	analysis	synthesis	evaluation
list	reword	use	examine	combine	decide
select	retell	solve	simplify	formulate	prioritize
name	explain	try	compare	make-up	classify
identify	project	develop	check	produce	arbitrate
underline	account for	manipulate	uncover	reorganize	accept/reject
identify	describe	perform	determine	predict	diagnose

- identify relevant information;
- draw conclusions; and
- evaluate information and sources.

Furthermore, a library & information skills curriculum based on Bloom's taxonomy provides a basis for offering learning experiences that increase the frequency with which students engage information at higher levels of thinking. Library & information skills instruction must be integrated with subject area classroom instruction. With a library & information skills curriculum emphasizing higher level skills, library media specialists and teachers are better able to design integrated activities that enable students to master a full range of information problem-solving skills.

Library & information skills and subject area curricula are combined in integrated unit and lesson plans. The information-related behaviors, questions and vocabulary (figures 10.2, 10.3 and 10.4) are all useful in designing and writing unit and lesson plans.

THE BIG SIX SKILLS CURRICULUM INTRODUCED

The *Big Six Skills* curriculum is dominated by (1) the information problem-solving approach and (2) Bloom's taxonomy of cognitive objectives. The sequence of the curriculum is the six steps of the information problem-solving process. The scope covers the full range of cognitive behaviors within each of the Big Six Skills areas. Therefore, the scope and sequence applies to every grade level and subject area. In each grade, instruction should first emphasize the Big Six Skills framework. Later, more specific skills development can be linked to students' levels of sophistication at that grade level. Similarly, learning activities and instruction can be coordinated and integrated with the real information needs and situations of subject area curriculum.

The Big Six Skills curriculum does appear to focus on the research concerns. However, the other areas typically found in library & information skills curriculum (reading guidance, literature appreciation, computer use and media production) are included within its scope.

Reading guidance and literature appreciation are traditional concerns of school library media programs. A full range of services associated with reading guidance has been described in chapter 9 as part of the curriculum support services function. Reading guidance and literature appreciation can also be viewed from an information problem-solving perspective. That is, students have classroom and personal information needs related to reading and literature. For example, a student may be seeking a work of fiction in a particular genre or time period to meet the specifications of an assignment. Another student may have read a book for recreational purposes and would like additional books by the same author or by others who write on similar subjects. Still another wants to know more about an author that was particularly impressive. These are all situations related to information problem-solving, and the Big Six Skills approach can be applied to meeting these needs. Thus, instructional activities designed to foster the reading habit, intellectual growth, and personal interests in literature and reading are highly appropriate to library & information skills instruction.

The areas of media and computer use are also included within the scope of the *Big Six Skills* curriculum. These areas are intended to give students competencies beyond the printed word and put students in a position to also be successful at accessing, using, and presenting information in a full variety of formats. Computers and media are increasingly important in information storage and retrieval. Computers also provide increased capabilities in analyzing, reformulating, and evaluating information. Therefore, media and computer use are equally important to each of the *Big Six Skills*.

The distinctions between the traditional approach to library skills instruction and the one presented here are three-fold: (1) this approach places isolated skills within an overall information problem-solving framework; (2) the emphasis is on developing transferable, higher level thinking skills; (3) the instruction is integrally linked to the general school curriculum. Thus, there is little value in teaching how to use the *Readers' Guide to Periodical Literature* in isolated library skills classes. In the Big Six Skills approach, the *Readers' Guide* should be taught, but only within the contexts of:

1. information problem-solving: an access and use skill to be used in certain information-seeking strategies to meet determined information needs;
2. Bloom's taxonomy: skill development beyond understanding to include application, analysis, synthesis and evaluation; and
3. subject area curriculum: tied to some real need of classroom instruction.

This approach is global in perspective yet can be specific in implementation. Success in implementation depends on consistently using a broad view of the information problem-solving process to teach basic as well as advanced skills.

Each area of the Big Six Skills curriculum deals with one of the stages in the problem-solving process and is attuned to the parameters of Bloom's taxonomy.

The Big Six Skills curriculum presents objectives in a systematic structure. For each of the six skills areas, there are a series of objectives designed to articulate those skills necessary and appropriate to attaining full competence in that general skill. Students must attain competence in preceding levels in order to gain skill at each successive level. Relating the Big Six Skills to subject area curriculum requires the articulation of *terminal objectives*. Terminal objectives are those integrated behaviors, jointly determined by library media specialists and classroom teachers, that demonstrate student competence in a given area. Related library & information skills objectives and classroom objectives can be considered as *enroute objectives*. Terminal objectives can be determined by grade level, program need, or subject area. The selection of terminal objectives are professional decisions, that should be determined within the context of curriculum development, program planning, and the total curriculum. The Big Six Skills curriculum should therefore be viewed as a framework to be modified and enhanced by each library media program to meet individual program and school curriculum needs.

The general information problem-solving model—the Big Six Skills—is the basic structure. Enroute and terminal objectives can be added, deleted or altered as indicated through an analysis of the curriculum and the needs of students. Adding or changing objectives should be consistent with the Big Six Skills structure and based on Bloom's taxonomy. It is useful to test objectives against the general description of each cognitive level (see figures 10.2 and 10.3). In this way, the Big Six Skills curriculum is individualized to local needs and becomes a realistic tool, useful for developing units of study and individual daily lesson plans.

The Big Six Skills curriculum is designed to help students become effective information problem-solvers. The goals are to have them approach every information problem with a systematic strategy and to think critically in finding, using, organizing, presenting, and evaluating information. Students with these skills should be more successful in dealing with an increasingly complex and information-rich world.

LIBRARY & INFORMATION SKILLS CURRICULUM
SCOPE AND SEQUENCE:
THE BIG SIX SKILLS

© EISENBERG & BERKOWITZ, 1987

The scope and sequence presented here is based on (1) a top-down approach to the information problem-solving process and (2) Bloom's taxonomy of cognitive skills.

Information problem-solving is viewed as a series of six broad skills areas: *The Big Six Skills*. The *sequence* therefore follows the logical order of the information problem-solving process. Within each area, there are specific skills objectives to be attained. These are outlined in hierarchical order based on Bloom's taxonomy of cognitive skills.

The *scope* of the curriculum is broad. It relates to any situation requiring information problem-solving and encompasses:

- the research process,
- media production,
- computer use,
- reading guidance, and
- literature appreciation.

Each of these areas are viewed within the framework of solving an information problem. Selecting a book for recreational reading, using a CD-ROM card catalog, writing a well-constructed thesis statement, producing a slide-tape show—these can all be considered as information problems. Instead of presenting these areas as separate sections of the curriculum, they are included here within a unified media concept.

We recognize that this approach to a scope and sequence differs from the traditional K-12 library skills curriculum. We feel that a simple curriculum, based on the information problem-solving process and presented within a critical thinking skills framework, makes conceptual sense and is relatively easy to implement.

The framework for the scope and sequence is as follows: Each of the Big Six Skills is first stated and then explained in terms of (1) a scope note, (2) examples, and (3) specific skills objectives presented in hierarchical order (knowledge, comprehension, application, analysis, synthesis, evaluation) with the associated level noted in brackets. The objectives are hierarchical in that if students achieve proficiency at a certain level within an area of the Big Six Skills, it can be assumed that all skills objectives under that level are also attained. For example, if under *information-seeking strategies* students are able to design a search strategy sequence to meet the needs of a defined information task—a synthesis-level skills objective—it can be assumed that students are able to meet all objectives related to information-seeking strategies prior to synthesis.

In order to emphasize the hierarchical nature of the taxonomy and the curriculum, the skills objectives are listed diagonally from right to left. As one scans down the page, those skills objectives at the higher levels appear more and more to the left.

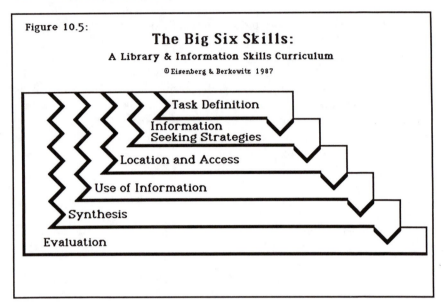

Figure 10.5.   The Big Six Skills: A Library & Information Skills Curriculum

GENERAL GOAL OF THE BIG SIX SKILLS CURRICULUM

Students will adopt a systematic approach to information problem-solving. At the highest level, this includes demonstrating the ability to evaluate the tasks relative to the *Big Six Skills*: (1) task definition, (2) information-seeking strategies, (3) location of and access to information, (4) use of information for a purpose, (5) synthesis in an appropriate form of presentation, and (6) evaluation of information, resources, strategies and procedures.

1. TASK DEFINITION

Scope Note

Task definition refers to determining the purpose and need for information. Definition of task is the required initial step in every information problem-solving situation. Before using any other information skill, students must first be able to articulate information needs.

Examples

Students may determine that in order to complete a particular homework assignment they need a chart not included in their textbooks; or they recognize that they must get a particular book representing a particular type of literature required for an English class; or they evaluate a thesis statement for a major research paper as complete.

Objectives

Students will demonstrate the ability to:

☐ list questions used to describe the information problem, e.g., *What do I need to know? Why do I need to know it? How will I know if my need is met?* [knowledge]

☐ explain the questions used for describing the information problem [comprehension]

☐ use the appropriate questions to determine the objective(s) of an information problem-solving situation [application]

☐ compare and confirm the objective(s) of an information problem-solving situation [analysis]

☐ formulate a complete statement of the information problem [synthesis]

☐ appraise the stated information problem: accept the statement and continue or reject the statement, reanalyze the situation, and reformulate the information problem statement [evaluation]

2. INFORMATION-SEEKING STRATEGIES

Scope Note

This group of skills refers to examining alternative approaches to the problems of acquiring appropriate information to meet defined tasks. These include recognizing various strategies for searching, comparing alternative strategies, selecting strategies appropriate for a defined task, and evaluating the selected strategy.

Examples

Students with an assignment (i.e., defined task) of writing a 3-page paper on the current political situation in Mexico would recognize the need for information beyond their personal knowledge or textbook; that sources to be considered include: current encyclopedias, periodicals, recent nonfiction books, and a current videocassette program on news broadcasts about Mexico.

Objectives

Students will demonstrate the ability to:

☐ list the choices in search stategy [knowledge]

☐ state in their own words search strategy choices [comprehension]

☐ use a chosen search strategy for a defined information task [application]

☐ examine search strategy choices for the requisite components [analysis]

☐ design a search strategy sequence to meet the needs of a defined information task [synthesis]

☐ evaluate a designed search strategy using criteria for an effective search strategy design [evaluation]

3. LOCATION OF AND ACCESS TO INFORMATION

Scope Note

Location is the ability to find a range of information sources to meet a defined information task. *Access* is the ability to retrieve sources as well as specific information from sources. Together, location and access skills refer to finding and retrieving information in the library media center, beyond the individual center (through networks and interlibrary loan), and within specific sources. While important, these skills are not the sum and total of a library & information skills program. Location and access must be viewed within the larger context of the information problem solving process.

Examples

Specific types of sources to be considered within location and access are listed in appendix A.

Objectives

Students will demonstrate the ability to:

☐ list the variety and range of available information resources; and the skills necessary to access information [knowledge]

☐ describe the range of information resources available [comprehension]

☐ locate and use a range of sources to gather information [application]

☐ examine the appropriateness of resources in solving an information task [analysis]

☐ develop a plan using a range of appropriate resources to locate and access information to carry out an information task [synthesis]

☐ determine whether or not the resources located and the information accessed fulfill the information task [evaluation]

4. USE OF INFORMATION

Scope Note

Use of information refers to the application of information to meet defined information tasks. With these skills, students move beyond location and access to being able to identify, analyze, and assess how well information meets a specific purpose.

Examples

Once a student has defined the task as requiring up-to-date information about stock market trends, and after locating and retrieving a periodical article about economic trends over the past two years, the student must be able to understand the charts, tables, and text as well as evaluate the reliability of the information contained within the source.

Objectives

Students will demonstrate the ability to:

☐ list the uses of information for defined tasks [knowledge]

☐ identify appropriate information from sources (see appendix A) [knowledge]

☐ explain the uses of information for defined tasks [comprehension]

☐ use information which has been accessed through reading, listening, observing for defined tasks [application]

☐ analyze accessed information to determine appropriate uses for defined tasks [analysis]

☐ integrate information drawn from a source into prior understandings about a topic [synthesis]

☐ judge the usefulness of information drawn from a source to meet defined tasks [evaluation]

5. SYNTHESIS

Scope Note

Synthesis refers to the ability to integrate information drawn from a range of sources. Synthesis brings together existing information and adds value to it by restructuring and repackaging the information to meet defined tasks. Synthesis also includes selecting appropriate formats for presentation of information, (i.e. various oral, written, or multimedia forms) and involves presenting information using the selected format and evaluating whether the format was effective in communicating the reformulated message.

Examples

The elementary student who looks at two books illustrated by the same person and draws a picture that could appear in either book is involved with synthesis. Synthesis also occurs when students use works of literary criticism and their own ideas to write papers on symbolism in *Moby Dick*.

Objectives

Students will demonstrate the ability to:

☐ identify formats for presenting information   [knowledge]

☐ explain formats for presenting information   [comprehension]

☐ show relationships between given information [application]

☐ determine appropriate formats for presenting information [analysis]

☐ present research findings using appropriate formats of presentation [synthesis]

☐ evaluate the presented research and the effectiveness of the used presentation format based on a set of predetermined criteria [evaluation]

6. EVALUATION

Scope Note

Evaluation involves making judgments based on a set of criteria. Evaluation here involves two aspects: (1) evaluation of the entire information problem-solving process (and each of the steps in the process), and (2) evaluation of whether the original task as defined was met.

Examples

Students conducting online searches will need to judge the effectiveness of their strategies by comparing the relevance of the citations retrieved to the original information need. Through evaluation, teams of students required to give persuasive speeches are able to determine whether they have adequate information for their points of view.

Objectives

Students will demonstrate the ability to:

☐ list the components of the information problem-solving process (the Big Six Skills) [knowledge]

☐ restate the components of the information problem-solving process [comprehension]

☐ make use of the Big Six Skills to determine how to research an information problem [application]

☐ examine a sample research procedure to determine which components of the information problem-solving process are included [analysis]

☐ construct a research procedure for a given information problem [synthesis]

☐ critique research procedures based on the criteria previously determined in the information problem solving process (e.g., answering the question "Did I successfully complete the defined task?") [evaluation]

The scope and sequence as presented translate theory into a do-able approach to library & information skills instruction. From an awareness of how to incorporate the cognitive levels theory into a library & information curriculum comes an understanding that access to information is not an end in and of itself. The levels of knowledge and comprehension are foundations to levels of thinking that students must master if they are to become intelligent information users and information creators at higher cognitive levels.

The hallmark of a valued program lies in the perception of its role within the school's purpose and overall educational goals. The *Big Six Skills* curriculum is central to the educational program. Developing specific curriculum objectives linked with content area objectives puts the library media program in a special position in the school. Having high expectations to match the high level skills needed by students in an information-oriented society yields strong library media programs: well-supported and highly valued.

CHAPTER 11

Unit Plans and Lesson Plans

This book has stressed the importance of teaching library & information skills within the context of classroom instruction. In order to accomplish this, the comprehensive five-year and one-year plans must be articulated on more operational levels. Operational-level plans are unit and lesson plans. This chapter will:

- discuss the design and development of unit plans and lesson plans that integrate subject area instruction and the *Big Six Skills* curriculum;
- offer a format for unit and lesson plan design; and
- present exemplary unit plans and lesson plans.

• • •

Throughout this book much consideration has been given to using a systematic strategy to integrate the library media curriculum-related functions to the curriculum of the classroom. This includes determining the curriculum priorities of the school and matching these priorities with appropriate curriculum support services and library & information skills instruction. In a top-down fashion, planning starts with comprehensive five-year and detailed one-year plans. In the one-year plan, specific units of the school's curriculum are identified as particularly appropriate for integration with specific areas of the *Big Six Skills* curriculum. The task of articulating how this is actually accomplished is the purpose of the unit and lesson plans.

A successful library & information skills curriculum calls for an organized approach to linking library & information skills with content area skills. Inherent in the library & information skills curriculum is the philosophy of empowering students with skills and abilities that transfer across the entire panorama of curriculum. The curriculum model of information problem-solving, presented as the Big Six Skills, is a generalizable, highly adaptable approach that is applicable to any information problem situation. The challenges are (1) to determine the best possible situations for integrated instruction and (2) to design quality integrated learning experiences. The first challenge has been addressed in the *Six-Stage Strategy* for library media curriculum program development. A process for meeting the challenge of designing integrated units and lessons is presented below.

A PROCESS FOR DEVELOPING INTEGRATED UNIT AND LESSON PLANS

Before actually writing specific unit and lesson plans, it is useful to review certain decisions made within the context of the Six-Stage Strategy. This review includes confirming, revising, and explaining in more detail the classroom curriculum units deemed appropriate for integration with library & information skills instruction and those Big Six Skills areas associated with each unit. Although these tasks can be accomplished by library media specialists, they are even more effective when coordinated with a school's existing curriculum design and development process. At the very least, teachers and administrators should be involved through the building-level planning group. In addition, individual teachers will be involved in writing specific unit and lesson plans.

A curriculum development process for creating integrated unit and lesson plans is outlined below. The process centers on tasks jointly carried out by library media specialists and classroom teachers or teaching teams. This insures that unit and lesson plans reflect a unified understanding of the purpose and the objectives of both subject area and library & information skills curriculum.

(1) Review and Confirm those Content Area Curriculum Units that Were Determined to be Best Suited for Coordination with Library & Information Skills Instruction.

The purpose of this step is to review the decisions made under program feasibility as to those units particularly appropriate for coordination with library & information skills instruction. These are the units that will be developed further and rewritten to include relevant library & information skills components. The intent here is to confirm the suitability of the units and make adjustments as necessary. Information about units is available from (1) the rough-draft priority list (from the feasibility analysis) and (2) the schedule of curriculum units (part of the one-year plan).

(2) Review the Subject Area Objectives of Designated Units.

Before writing a unit from an integrated perspective, there must be a clear understanding of the subject area objectives for the unit. As it is likely that the units have existed for a number of years, objectives can be ascertained from existing unit and lesson plans as well as by consulting with teachers involved with the unit. The purpose is to reaffirm the subject area instructional objectives to insure that they will continue to be met.

(3) Review the Big Six Skills Associated with Each Designated Unit.

It is the intersection of the subject area objectives and the Big Six Skills that provides the best opportunities for instruction. Therefore, with the subject area objectives reaffirmed, the next step is to determine objectives from a library & information skills perspective. In addition to the overall information problem-solving process, there are specific Big Six Skills objectives to be stressed within the context of each unit. Initial decisions were made during feasibility and one-year planning stages. The *skills-by-unit* matrix documents initial decisions made regarding Big Six Skills and associated units. The task is to review these decisions and revise as appropriate. The linking of objectives from two different areas is one of the creative aspects of curriculum development. Care should be taken to insure that the Big Six Skills curriculum is adequately covered and linked to appropriate units.

(4) Establish Priorities for Developing Units.

This step first involves identifying the major considerations in establishing priorities and then using those considerations to determine the order in which units will be developed. Factors that may influence priority-setting include: (1) state and local mandates, (2) time frame and schedule, (3) established district or building-level priorities, (4) familiarity with the material and/or subject area, (5) relationships with teachers involved, the importance of the unit in the overall curriculum, (6) the availability of supporting material and services, and (7) the anticipated ease of unit development. By weighing these and other factors, unit writing can be planned and scheduled. This is important for coordinating efforts of teachers, library media specialists, and support staff.

(5) Write Unit Plans.

The unit plan presents the overall course of instruction by outlining the unit objectives, actions, methods, and resources. The unit plan describes the sequence of events, groups components of instruction, and provides the structure and context for daily lessons. Unit plans for integrated library & information skills instruction must cover components of both the subject area and library & information skills curricula.

Effective unit plans answer the questions:

- What is to be taught?
- To whom will it be taught?
- How it is to be taught?

- Who will teach what?
- When will it be taught?
- How will the the learning be evaluated?

A format for unit plans is outlined later in this chapter.

(6) Write daily lesson plans.

The daily lesson plan helps the library media specialist and classroom teacher coordinate the specific unit objectives. It accounts for the day-to-day details of what will be taught, how it will be taught, and how the learning will be evaluated. Daily lessons are framed within the unit plan and must provide continuity and flexibility. The level of specificity in lesson plans will depend upon local considerations. Some teachers and library media specialists will require details on every aspect of content and process. For others, an outline will suffice. The same questions asked for unit plans apply to lesson plans, that is,

- What is to be taught?
- To whom will it be taught?
- How it is to be taught?
- Who will teach what?
- When will it be taught?
- How will the the learning be evaluated?

A format for lesson plans is outlined later in this chapter.

(7) Review and confirm schedule for units.

After creating unit and lesson plans, the time sequence of instruction needs to be reviewed, revised, and confirmed. The original one-year plan included a *schedule of selected curriculum units*. Based upon the completed unit and lesson plans, the schedule is updated and revised. In unit and lesson design, consideration is given to the sequence of lessons, the needs of the students, the difficulty of concepts and tasks, the level of instruction, and the need for evaluation. These factors as well as the interrelationships of units, grade levels and subject areas all affect time frame and mandate reassessment of initial estimates and adjustments in schedule.

A FORMAT FOR UNIT PLANS

The unit format outline is a means of carefully organizing the information necessary for effective instructional unit plans. Unit plans need to be clear, concise and complete. A good unit plan is a usable document.

Figure 11.1:

Unit Plan Format

Name: Audience:

Overview:

Rationale:

Objectives:
   [Big Six Skills and Content Area Skills]

	Time	Accountability	Location

Planning Time:

Content/Activities:

Materials:

Evaluation:

Follow-up/
Alternative Activities:

Bibliography:

Figure 11.1.   Unit Plan Format

Name of Unit: The name or title of the instructional unit should clearly indicate its relationship to specific topics within the content area curriculum and, if possible, to the Big Six Skills curriculum.

Audience: The grade level, subject area, and/or specific classes for whom the unit is intended.

Overview: This is a brief summary of the nature and scope of the unit and should be no more than one paragraph in length.

Rationale: The rationale is the justification for the unit. It states why the unit was selected and the connection between the subject area curriculum and the library & information skills curriculum.

Objective(s): Both content area and library & information skills objectives are listed. Objectives can be listed separately or together with specific reference to the Big Six Skills curriculum and subject area curriculum.

Content Outline: A general outline of the subject area material to be covered with notations of related library & information skills material. Content, activities, time frame, accountability, and location are all presented together in figure 11.1

Suggested Activities/Procedures: A major section of the unit plan is the designation of suggested activities. These are recommendations and alternatives for accomplishing the unit objective(s). Within a unit consideration must be given to:

- introductory, major, and concluding activities;
- sequential arrangement of activities;
- time associated with each activity; and
- evaluation procedures.

The suggested activities/procedures note the teaching methods and styles to be employed. In the overall unit plan, other components (content, time, accountability, and location) are linked to suggested activities.

Accountability: There needs to be a notation of instructional roles and responsibilities of individuals for teaching or assisting in the implementation of the daily lessons and how time will be allocated for each activity.

Location: For each activity, there should be an indication of the location of the instruction: library media center, classroom, or other location (e.g., public or college library, computer lab, television studio).

Teaching Materials: Specific materials and equipment (book, reference, periodical, nonprint, audiovisual, computer) that will be used to teach the unit. If desired, materials can be linked with associated content and activities.

Planning Time: The amount of time necessary and appropriate for the joint development by the library media specialist and content area teacher or teaching team. Can refer to entire unit planning or be broken down by daily lessons or selected activity.

Evaluation: Methods for determining the extent to which students have accomplished the unit objectives. Includes both subject area and library & information skills evaluation techniques.

Follow-Up Activities: Optional, alternative or suggested activities to reinforce or extend student learning. These are particularly useful if a link can be established to other library & information skills units.

Bibliography: The sources of information used to create the unit plan.

Unit plans provide continuity and direction for the coordinated, integrated library & information skills instruction program. It is necessary to include information in each of the categories noted above. As much as possible, unit plans need to be practical and based on realistic expectations.

A FORMAT FOR LESSON PLANS

Unit design provides structure and direction for lesson design. The daily lesson plan format outlined below offers a framework that isolates and carefully organizes individual objectives into their integral parts for daily presentation . Daily lesson plans translate the overall objectives, content, and activities of the unit plan into specific daily events. Additionally, lesson plans provide a means for adding specificity necessary to meet the needs of individual classes. Lesson plans must be flexible and able to change based on the progress and accomplishments of prior lessons.

Lesson Name: This should be clearly and concisely written. If possible, the name should set the lesson within an integrated unit and more general curriculum context.

Unit Context: The unit associated with the lesson.

Audience: The appropriate grade level(s) and subject area(s) for the lesson.

Topic: A brief summary of the lesson from the subject area curriculum perspective.

Big Six Skills Area: A brief explanation of the lesson from the library & information skills perspective.

Objective(s): Both the subject area and library & information skills learning objectives to be covered in the lesson.

Level of Instruction: Notation as to whether the instruction concerns introduction of new material or concepts; review, remediation, or reinforcement; or expansion and enhancement. The level may influence the number of objectives that can be approached within any one lesson.

Content/Activity/Presentation: A statement of what is going to be covered and what is going to be done by the instructors and by the students. This is the central section of the daily lesson plan and describes the specific content, sequence, and time frame of learning activities designed to meet stated objectives.

Figure 11.2:
Lesson Plan Format

Lesson Name: Audience:

Topic:

Unit Context:

Level of Instruction:

Big Six Skills Area:

Objective(s):
   [Big Six Skills and Content Area Skills]

Time	Accountability	Location

Content/Activities:

Materials:

Evaluation:

Resources:

Special Conerns:

Figure 11.2.   Lesson Plan Format

As with the unit plan, this section includes more specificity on the content, methodology, time frame, accountability, and location of the lesson.

Materials: The list of all instructional and library media materials necessary for the lesson. This component is a crucial link between subject area and library & information skills curricula. Materials includes those resources to be used by students, teachers, and the library media specialists.

Evaluation: This refers to the measurement of students' performance. It is important to evaluate both subject area and library & information skills objectives. The challenge is to devise evaluation techniques that meet the needs of both areas.

Special Concerns: This is a catch-all section where the library media specialist or teacher can include anecdotal information, concerns, or special questions to be considered when implementing and evaluating the lesson. Special concerns might include questions about:

- timing;
- appropriateness of activities;
- pre-test/post-test;
- flexibility;
- motivation;
- relevance;
- the relationship to other lessons in the unit.

Systematic presentation of information on the basic elements of a lesson will help insure success in instruction. It is important that lesson plans be simple, concise, and focused on the unit objectives.

• • •

The formats presented for unit and lesson plans are intended as recommendations. The structure and layout of the plans are less important than the content included. Specific labels may change, but the components or types of information to include is essentially the same.

Whether or not you use these particular formats, it is important to recognize the need for written instruction plans based on both the library & information skills and the content area curricula. Unit and lesson plans must include and follow from stated subject area and library & information skills objectives. Structured unit and lesson plans insure a systematically integrated library and information skills instructional program.

The underlying strength in the process is the planning, partnership, and working relationships established with teachers (or teaching teams). Well-conceived plans, developed and organized jointly with subject area teachers create opportunities to meet the needs of students and strengthen the position of the library media center instructional program within the total school curriculum.

The concluding section of this chapter offers detailed exemplary unit plans and specific lesson plans based on the Six-Stage Strategy and the planning formats described above.

EXEMPLARY ELEMENTARY UNIT

Unit: Appreciating and Writing Biography*

Audience: 5th Grade

Goal: The goal of this unit is to introduce children to the literary form of biography. When this unit of study is completed, students will be able to identify it, can write a brief biography based on information accessed through an interview, and understand that the genre of biography is important.

Rationale: It is valuable to appreciate the biography, as a means of gaining insight into people, their methods and motivations, decisions and directions, failures and successes, and their influence on their world and the world of others. Within the context of Language Arts, students will learn the characteristics of the biography as a literary form. Students will come to value biography as a recreational reading alternative.

Objectives:

Students will demonstrate the ability to:

1. identify a work of literatuare as a biography;
    (Task Definition)
2. define "biography" as defined by the library media specialist, and also be able to explain the definition in their own words;
    (Task Definition)
3. understand that one way to access biographical information is through conducting an interview;
    (Information Seeking Strategy)
4. apply the process of creating a biography;
    (Synthesis)

_____

* Special thanks to Judith Gordon for her contributions in the design of the elementary unit and lesson.

5. determine if the characteristics of a biography are exhibited in a given example;
    (Evaluation)
6. write a biography from information accessed through an interview.
    (Synthesis)

Content/Activities:

Part I—Looking at Biographies—(to understand what makes a work of literature a biography, and to examine a work of literature and identify it as biography)

1. Define biography as bio = life and graphy = recording.
    Read a portion of a biography aloud to the class.
    Ask students discussion questions such as: What did you learn about (the person)? What makes this a biography? [1.5 periods]
2. Get a biography from library media center. [0.5 period]
3. Read the selected biography silently.
    In reading groups or, as a class, have the students read silently. After reading, make a list of the characteristics of a biography found in the reading. [2 periods]
4. Review the definition of "biography".
    As a class, share list of the characteristics of a biography. [1 period]
5. Examine a biography.
    Each student should take the list of characteristics, and examine it to identify the characteristics of a biography found in their book. [homework]

Part II—Writing a Biography—(to understand that one way to create a biography is from information accessed through a personal interview)

6. Information Seeking Strategy for writing a biography.
    Have students complete the *Information Seeking Strategy Worksheet for Writing a Biography.* [0.5 period]
7. Plan to interview a person in order to gather information to write a biography. Announce to the students that a "special guest" will be in the media center tomorrow and tell them that they, as a group, are going to write a biography of him or her. Using the completed worksheet from step 6, and the list of biography elements from Part I, generate a list of questions to ask the guest personality. [0.5 period]
8. Conduct the interview.
    Students will interview the "special guest" using the list of questions they developed in step 7. (NOTE: it may be helpful to have a cassette recording of the session for students to refer to later.) [1 period]
9. Use the information accessed from the interview.

Students will compile the notes from the interview and determine if: a) they asked the questions they had prepared, b) their questions were answered, and c) they asked the questions and got the answers they need in order to write a biography. [homework]

10. Review the information accessed from the interview.
    Students will review the information obtained by interviewing the "special guest".
    Students will also be able to ask questions of each other to gain information they may have missed. [1 period]

11. Students may listen to the tape of the interview to gain additional information (independent work in the library media center).

12. Prepare an outline.
    Students write an outline of the key points about the guest from which a short biography will be prepared. [1 period]

13. Write a short biography.
    Based on activites 8, 9, 10, 11, & 12 students will write a short biography of the "special guest." [homework]

14. Examine the biography of the "special guest."
    Students will evaluate the biographies they wrote based on the criteria established for biographies in activities 1, 3, and 4.
    Interview a classmate to gather information in order to write a biography. Students make a list of interview questions to ask classmates. Students conduct classmate interviews.
    Students compile their information. [2 periods]

15. Write a biography of a classmate.
    Students write short classmate biographies.
    Students share and evaluate their work. (What did you learn about your classmate that you didn't know before? In what ways does the biography you wrote meet the definition of biography?)
    [homework; 1 period in class]

Planning Time: The library media specialist and the classroom teacher will need approximately 1 hour of joint planning time to coordinate the activities for this unit of study. Each will need approximately 1 hour: the library media specialist to gather the needed resources for both library media specialist's lessons and the teacher's and to invite a "special guest"; the teacher to prepare for the classmate biographies.

Accountability:

	Activities	Place	Primary Teacher	Assisting Teacher	L.I.S.	Periods
part I	1	LMC	LMS	T	1	1.5
	2	LMC	LMS	—	2,3	0.5
	3	C	T	—	4,5,6	2
	4	C	T	LMS	4,5,6	1
	5	—	—	—	1,2,6	homework
part II	6	LMC	LMS	T	2	0.5
	7	LMC	LMS	—	2	0.5
	8	LMC	LMS	—	3,4	1
	9	—	—	—	3,5,6	homework
	10	C	T	LMS	3,5,6	1
	11	LMC	—	—	3,5,6	indep. work
	12	C	T	—	4,5	1
	13	—	—	—	4,5	homework
	14	C	T	—	2,6	2
	15	C	T	LMS	4,5,6	homework;1

LMC = Library Media Center
C   = Classroom
LMS = Library Media Specialist
T   = Classroom Teacher
L.I.S. = Big Six Library & Information Skills Objectives:
     1 = task definition
     2 = information seeking strategy
     3 = location and access
     4 = use of information
     5 = synthesis
     6 = evaluation

Evaluation Procedures:

Students will demonstrate the ability to:

1. recall the definition of biography and explain the definition in their own words. Students will participate in the discussions in activities 1, 3, 4, & 5, and successfully complete the worksheet for activity 6.
2. apply the process of creating a biography by compiling the information from an interview of a guest and writing a short biography in activities 9 - 13. (group introductory activity)
3. conduct an interview of a classmate, and write a short biography of the classmate in activities 14 & 15. (individual guided practice activity)
4. evaluate the written biographies in activities 14 & 15 based on established criteria.
5. tell in their own words the process for writing a biography from an interview.

Teaching Materials:

Information Seeking Strategy Worksheet (see attached)
markers and chart paper
cassette tape recorder & tape
invited "special guest"

Alternative Activities:

1. Show a biographic videocassette or 16mm movie, and discuss the elements of biography.
2. Teacher or library media specialist dress up as a famous person students might "recognize".

EXEMPLARY ELEMENTARY LESSON

Lesson Plan: Activity 7

Unit: Appreciating and Writing Biography

Audience: 5th Grade

Objective: Students will participate in making a list of questions to use when interviewing the "special guest". The information accessed in this lesson will be used to write a short biography. (see Appreciating and Writing Biography—unit plan activity 8).

Methodology: The library media specialist will conduct this lesson using discussion technique. The lesson will be held in the library media center, with the assistance of the classroom teacher.

1. Tell students that a "special guest" is coming to the library media center and that they will interview the person in order to write a short biography.
2. Have students tell what they already know about the guest, if anything. Have students tell where they found that information.
3. Ask students to look at their worksheets from activity 6 and the list of characteristics of biography from Part I—activities 1, 2 & 3 and, decide what else they need to learn about the guest.
4. Compile students' interview questions from the *Information Seeking Strategy Worksheet for Writing a Biography*. Discuss, based on what they have learned about biographies, which answered questions will help them the most when writing the "special guest's" biography.
5. Review list—eliminate repeats.
6. Each student should be prepared to ask the "special guest" at least one question.
7. Have each student write his or her question on a separate sheet of paper, leaving room to write the "special guest's" answer. Pair students so that when one asks a question, the other writes the response.

Evaluation: The students will demonstrate their information seeking strategy abilities by participating in making the list of questions which, when answered, will provide enough information to write a biography, and knowing they can access the needed information through interviewing the special guest.

Materials: List of biography elements from activities 1, 3, & 4

Completed *Information Seeking Strategy Worksheet for Writing a Biography* worksheets from activity 6

Writing paper and pencils
Chart paper and markers

INFORMATION SEEKING STRATEGY WORKSHEET:
INTERVIEWING FOR A BIOGRAPHY

Name: _____ Class: _____

1. Write 3 questions that will help you find out about a person's childhood.
   [example: date of birth, schools, favorite toys, favorite teacher, hero]

   _____

   _____

   _____

2. List 3 things you'd like to know about the person as a young adult.
   [example: hero, first job, how they decided on a career]

   _____

   _____

   _____

3. List 3 things you'd like to know about the person's family.
   [example: parents, brothers & sisters, children, favorite family activity]

   _____

   _____

   _____

4. Write 3 "What if" questions to help find out more about the person.
   [example: What would you be if you couldn't be a _____?
            How would you change the world if you had one wish?]

   _____

   _____

   _____

EXEMPLARY SECONDARY UNIT

Integrated Teaching Unit—English 4 / Library & Information Skills

Unit:	Persuasive Speech*
Audience:	English 4
Overview:	This unit extends students' library and information skills in using both print and nonprint formats. Student success requires the development of a product, media supported persuasive speech, based on integrated classroom, library media center, and independent activities.
Rationale:	Oral communication for purposes of persuasion is a highly valuable, though often intimidating skill, useful in students' academic, business and personal lives. Preparation for effective persuasive communication involves information problem-solving as well as a full range of public speaking techniques. Media support, when carefully planned and fully integrated with the purpose of the speech, contributes significantly to the clarity and persuasiveness of the oral presentation.
General Objective:	Students will demonstrate the ability to prepare and deliver persuasive speeches on topics of their choice. An integral part of each speech will be a student produced nonprint media component.

Big Six Skills Objectives:

1. Task Definition   Students will demonstrate the ability to:
   - define their topics
   - define their audience
   - define the purpose of their speech
   - determine the information needed
2. Information Seeking Strategies   Students will demonstrate the ability to:
   - identify possible sources of information
   - prioritize sources for search purposes

---

* Special thanks to Gail Bieszad for her contributions in the design of the secondary unit and lesson.

3. Location & Access — Students will demonstrate the ability to:
    - obtain a variety of pertinent information from a variety of sources

4. Use of Information — Students will demonstrate the ability to:
    - determine the relevancy, point of view, and reliability of their information
    - select appropriate materials for their chosen media support

5. Synthesis — Students will demonstrate the ability to:
    - combine and organize materials for speech
    - write speech
    - edit and rewrite speech as necessary
    - prepare appropriate media for presentation support
    - present speech with media support.

6. Evaluation — Students will demonstrate the ability to:
    - complete evaluation sheet for own speech
    - complete evaluation sheets for 2 speeches by classmates (as assigned by teacher).

Unit Organization:

Period	Accountability	Location	Big Six Skills*
1	T	C	1
	LMS (T	LMC	1,2,3
2	assists)	LMC	1,4
	LMS (T	LMC &	2,3,4,5
3/4	assists)	C	2,3,4,5,6
5/6/7	LMS & T		2,3,4,5,6
8/9	LMS (T assist)	LMC	5
2 wks	T & LMS	C	6
10–14	T	C	
15	T & LMS		

* Big Six Skills relate both to the information and the media support components in this instructional unit.

[NOTE: A minimum of 1 period should be allocated as joint planning time with the classroom teacher, and a minimum of 2 periods should be allocated for setting up audiovisual stations, and review of video taped speeches.]

LMC = Library Media Center
C   = Classroom
LMS = Library Media Specialist
T   = Classroom Teacher
Big Six Skills—Library & Information Skills:
  1 = task definition
  2 = information seeking strategy
  3 = location and access
  4 = use of information
  5 = synthesis
  6 = evaluation

Content/Activities: Period 1:
General Discussion of Unit to be studied.
Discussion of required assignments to be completed by students.
Discussion of persuasive speeches; definition, purposes, likely audiences; techniques.
Brainstorming for topics.

Period 2:
Review assignment.
Demonstrate example(s) of media supported persuasive speech
Topic selection.
Brief review of information sources.

Periods 3-4:
Review and reinforce media support requirements.
Discussion and demonstration of available media support materials—including characteristics and appropriate use of nonprint media, and common errors in use of media.

Periods 5-7:
Library Media Center research—use of resources (small groups in class and Library Media Center as needed).

Periods 8-9:
Research.
Selection of appropriate media support.
Media production.

Two weeks: production of media support material (independent work)

Periods 10-14:
Speech presentations (videotaped).
Evaluation sheets completed.

LMS reviews videotaped speeches.

Period 15:
In class discussion and evaluation of speeches and media
support techniques.

*Evaluation
Method:*   Combined grade from Library Media Specialist (40%) and
                     Teacher (60%). Grade based on: (1) student's achievement
                     of Big Six Skills objectives, (2) overall quality and effec-
                     tiveness of his media support materials, (3) evaluation
                     sheets, and (4) overall impression of the persuasive speech.

Possible   Follow- 1. Have students watch a political debate, a presidential
up Activities: address, or a telethon and evaluate the presentation for
                         persuasiveness. Particular note should be made of me-
                         dia support (or lack of media support) and its
                         effectiveness.
                     2. Arrange for a media supported sales presentation by
                         local professional for students observation, discussion
                         and evaluation.
                     3. Review an industrial sales training film.
                     4. Have each student choose and view a television com-
                         mercial. Evaluate for persuasiveness and use of visual
                         and audio images.

Materials: (on reserve in the Library Media Center for students)

_____. "AV Equipment Self-Instruction Packets." Westminster, Md; Random House,
     undated.
Kemp, Jerrold E. *Planning and Producing Audiovisual Materials.* NY: Harper & Row.
     1980.
Minor, Ed and Frey, Harry. *Techniques for Producing Visual Instructional Materials.*
     NY: McGraw Hill Book Co. 1977.
Oates, S.C. *Audio Visual Equipment Self-Instructional Manual.* NY: I.C. Brown. 1979.
Thomas, James L. *Nonprint Production for Students, Teachers and Media Specialists.*
     Littleton Colorado: Libraries Unlimited, Inc. 1982.

Bibliography:

————. "AV Equipment Self-Instruction Packets." Westminster, Md; Random House, undated.

Kemp, Jerrold E. *Planning and Producing Audiovisual Materials.* NY: Harper & Row. 1980.

Minor, Ed and Frey, Harry. *Techniques for Producing Visual Instructional Materials.* NY: McGraw Hill Book Co. 1977.

Oates, S.C. *Audio Visual Equipment Self-Instructional Manual.* NY: I.C. Brown. 1979.

O'Malley, C.O. " Driving Your Point Home." *Personal Computers.* 10:86 (August 1986).

O'Malley, C.O. "Graphics: Visual Business Presentations." Personal Computers. 10:105 (October 1986).

Thomas, James L. *Nonprint Production for Students, Teachers and Media Specialists.* Littleton Colorado: Libraries Unlimited, Inc. 1982.

Wilbur, L. Perry. *Stand Up—Speak Up—or Shut Up.* NY: Dember Books, 1981.

EVALUATION FORM
MEDIA SUPPORTED PERSUASIVE SPEECH

Speaker: _____

Speech: _____

Evaluator: _____

Rate the persuasive speech from 1 (lowest rating) to 10 (highest rating) in each of the following areas:

_____ 1   Content (information was well chosen, and to the point)

_____ 2   Clarity (information was well organized and understandable)

_____ 3   Oral Presentation (delivery was smooth, clear, and comfortable)

_____ 4   Media Content (media support was well chosen, and appropriate)

_____ 5   Media Presentation (media use was effective and used with ease)

_____ 6   Overall Persuasiveness (the speech "did the job")

Please comment on the effective and/or impressive parts of this persuasive presentation.

Please comment on the areas in which the persuasive presentation could have been improved.

EXEMPLARY SECONDARY LESSON

Name: Persuasive Speech

Lesson Plan: Periods 3 & 4

Audience: English 4

Unit Context: This lesson introduces students to the nonprint media sup-
                   port possibilities to meet the requirements of their persua-
                   sive speech.

Period	Accountability	Location	Big Six Skills
3/4	LMS (T assists)	LMC*	1, 4

* Audio Visual Production Center if available

Topic: Review media support requirements for persuasive speech.
                   Introduce students to appropriate and available media.

Objectives: (1) Students will explain to a classmate how to use the
                        audiovisual equipment at each learning station.
                   (2) Students will select appropriate media to be used
                        within the persuasive speech as an aid to support point
                        of view.
                   (3) Using criteria given by the library media specialist,
                        students will explain why their selected media support
                        is appropriate.

Content/Activities: (1) Review media support requirements for the persua-
                            sive speech.
                       (2) Discuss and demonstrate advantages and disadvan-
                            tages of various methods of nonprint media support
                            including:

a) necessary equipment
b) logistic
c) lighting requirements
d) limitations on effective use
e) software production requirements and methods
f) necessary lead-time for production
g) cost
h) frequent user errors

NOTE: Include (minimally) overhead projector, slide projector, audio cassette recorder, record player, video cassette recorder, 35mm camera and copy stand, chart and easel, and filmstrip.

(3) Students go to media stations (previously set up) to experience and practice using the various media formats.

(4) Encourage students to use reserve shelf books on media methods and production before deciding which media support method to use.

(5) Homework assignment
Read: O'Malley, C.O. "Driving Your Point Home." *Personal Computers.* 10:86 (August 1986).

Materials: Appropriate audiovisual equipment and software for demonstrations and stations. Reading assignment handouts.

Evaluation: Assessment of student participation in discussions and demonstrations. *Selection of Appropriate Media Worksheet.*

Special Needs: Those schools without special audiovisual facilities will need 3 or 4 students to assist in setting up media equipment stations (in the library media center or classroom) before class and to take down after class. Those library media programs with audiovisual centers or special areas available will handle this aspect differently.

SELECTION OF APPROPRIATE MEDIA—WORKSHEET

Name:

Class:

Date/Period:

Topic: _____

Thesis Statement: _____

_____

_____

General Approach to Speech: _____

_____

_____

_____

_____

	Media:	Purpose
1	_____	_____
2	_____	_____
3	_____	_____

[Note: Students must use at least one, but no more than three different media support items.]

Estimate of time required to create media support items _____

CHAPTER 12

A Look to the Future

In this final chapter, the major themes of the book are reviewed and reasserted. Successful delivery of the major curriculum-related functions insure that the library media program is an active, integral part of the entire educational program. The responsibilities associated with curriculum support services go far beyond simply providing resources. They encompass a wide range of activities including reading guidance, information service, curriculum consultation, and curriculum development. Likewise, library & information skills instruction involves much more than teaching location and access skills. Students need to attain skills in the full information problem-solving process. To fulfill curriculum support services and library & information skills functions, this book has focused on systematic development of curricula, systems, and activities through the Six-Stage Strategy.

The chapter concludes with a look to the future. In the near future, one can envision the library media program as the center for content-based learning. This is a logical extension of successful support services and skills instruction functions with active library media specialists totally involved in the curriculum-development process. Looking to the more distant future, the trends and predictions for life-long, decentralized, technology-driven, and increasingly information-based education all have major implications for library media programs. It seems clear that information-oriented curriculum support services will play a major, crucial role in future educational programs. Likewise, information problem-solving will be emphasized as a basic skill, pervading the entire curriculum.

CURRICULUM CONCERNS OF THE LIBRARY MEDIA PROGRAM

This book has stressed a number of points relating to the role and functions of the library media program:

- the curriculum concerns of the library media program can be grouped under two major functions: (1) curriculum support services and (2) library & information skills instruction;
- education today increasingly requires a range of information-oriented curriculum support services;
- instruction in library & information skills should focus on developing a logical, critical-thinking approach to information problem-solving;

149

- both curriculum support services and library & information skills instruction must be based on the real curriculum as taught; and
- the key to creating a program of effective curriculum-related functions is adoption of a systematic planning strategy.

The library media program is centrally involved in the school's curriculum program in two ways: (1) by providing necessary curriculum support services, and (2) by integrating instruction in information problem-solving with classroom instruction. While certain aspects of these two functions might be emphasized differently from school to school, significant involvement in both is essential. That is, curriculum support services and library & information skills instruction are required components of every active library media program.

In this book, the phrase *curriculum support services* is used to describe a wide range of meaningful curriculum-related activities. It is an umbrella term encompassing five service areas: resources provision, reading guidance, information service, curriculum consultation, and curriculum development. Through curriculum support services, the library media specialist provides leadership and direction in curriculum design and delivery, and in the way information is used. Within this broad, highly-involved context, the terms *service* and *support* are viewed as valued, vital, foundations for effective teaching.

Regarding *library & information skills instruction*, the emphasis is clearly beyond teaching location and access skills. The Big Six Skills curriculum is designed to assist students in developing skills associated with information problem-solving. In their schoolwork and personal lives, students are continually faced with problems related to information. This is true in all grades: K–12. Students need to adopt and use, a systematic approach to information problem-solving. At the highest level, students need to be able to evaluate their effectiveness in information problem-solving and improve their skills as necessary.

For most of this book, the dual functions of curriculum support services and library & information skills instruction have been considered separately. Convergence was noted in three areas: (1) the articulation of plans, (2) reading guidance, and (3) the development of major skills instruction units. Planning involves articulating and scheduling the components of a program. Therefore, for the library media program, the schedules and matrices must be concerned with both library & information skills instruction and curriculum support services. The connections and relationships among the elements of these two functions become apparent through the planning process.

Reading guidance has been explained from both a support service and a library & information skills perspective. Promotion of literature, literacy, and reading are major concerns throughout the school's curriculum. The library media specialist is just one teacher among many providing direct educational opportunites to students to develop reading skills. Therefore, in addition to providing direct reading guidance activities to students, the library media specialist must offer a range of reading guidance support services to classroom teachers involved with reading guidance.

Finally, an integrated approach to library & information skills requires both curriculum support services and skills instruction by definition. Integrated units are clearly part of the library & information skills curriculum. However, creation of these units requires a cooperative effort by library media specialists, teachers, and administrators. In this capacity, the library media specialist is providing valuable curriculum development services. Therefore, the design of major coordinated units is part of both functions: curriculum support services and library & information skills instruction.

While the convergence of the two functions may be apparent in these and other specific situations, the overall question of the relationship of these two roles is not fully resolved. The conceptual question remains:

"Does the library media program involve two fairly distinct functions or are they somehow tied together under one, pervading purpose?"

All information systems—libraries, information centers, bibliographic retrieval systems, card catalogs—exist to assist people in meeting their information needs. The common purpose of these systems is to get patrons in touch with the information or sources of information necessary to meet their information problems. For the most part, libraries and other information systems have met this challenge by providing a range of services to patrons. These services often take the form of (1) providing collections and access tools (including automated retrieval systems), and (2) having information professionals (e.g., librarians) available to assist patrons in finding, collecting, evaluating, and using relevant information. The focus has clearly been on service, and it is only recently that the words "training" and "education" are commonly heard in university libraries and corporate and government settings.

The library media program shares the same overall purpose as other libraries and information systems. It exists to assist users in meeting their information needs. However, while other library and information situations focus on services, library media programs have tended, traditionally, to focus on instruction in library & information skills. This is not surprising as the library media program exists in an educational context.

Most other information systems deal with immediate, short-term situations. A user approaches the system with a problem; the system goes to work; the information is provided; the need is met; and the interaction is ended. However, the concerns of the library media program go beyond immediate, specific problems and interactions. As educators, library media specialists have a responsibility to anticipate the future needs of their patrons and to consider the ability of students to resolve their information problems in the future.

What can be anticipated in terms of information service and assistance in settings other than schools? Information service in various settings in society is haphazard and inconsistent. In some situations, a full range of information resources and support is available along with trained, competent information professionals. In others, one may not even find an up-to-date collection of resources. And even in school environments, the variability in staffing patterns and resources is so great that there is little consistency even within school districts or regions. For these reasons, it is natural that rather than continually meet short-term information needs, school library media specialists have chosen to emphasize the preparation of students to be independent users of libraries and information resources.

In addition to instructing students in library & information skills, library media specialists are directly involved with meeting the information needs of patrons through a full range of curriculum support services. This involvement takes the form of direct, immediate assistance as well as more long-term planning and design activities. Library media specialists are directly involved with assisting students and teachers in acquiring and using relevant information through the activities associated with resources provision, reading guidance, and information service. Each of these areas includes a series of meaningful services that actively provide materials. For example, resources provision involves assessing information needs, gathering appropriate materials, and determining the best way to make the materials available. Similarly, reading guidance assumes active interaction of the library media specialist with students and teachers. And information service means just that—providing teachers, administrators, and students with direct information.

Library media specialists also deal with information needs from a planning and design perspective by providing leadership in determining how information is to be used in curriculum. Curriculum involves the interactions of learning objectives, processes and resources. Through curriculum consultation and curriculum development, the library media specialist is able to influence what is expected from students and how information, resources, and systems are to be used. This is a significant expansion of responsibilites and places the library media specialist at the center of curriculum. In a very real sense, through curriculum support services the library media specialist is able to help to define the information needs of students.

It is clear that curriculum support services and library & information skills instruction both contribute to fulfilling the overall purpose of the library media program: to meet the information needs of users, now and in the future. To be effective, both areas must expand beyond traditional approaches. Library media specialists must work with teachers to (1) design units and lessons that challenge students to develop proficiency at information problem-solving while meeting subject area objectives, and (2) determine and meet the information needs of curricula. As this is easier to state than accomplish in real school settings, a major portion of this book is devoted to considering how to to bring about development in both curriculum support services and library & information skills instruction. The Six-Stage Strategy was conceived and designed as a realistic approach to fulfilling the need for a systematic approach to meeting curriculum-related needs.

THE SHORT-TERM FUTURE

Chapter 2 examined the changes and developments in the role of the library media specialist over the past twenty-five years. Three major trends were noted:

1. an expansion of functions;
2. a move from passive to active involvement; and
3. a conflict in perceptions.

An expansion of functions refers to the addition of new responsibilities and growth in traditional areas. At this point in time, the overall framework and direction for curriculum involvement is reasonably set. It is probable, however, that specific new services, activities, media, collections, and systems will arise in the near future. Fulfilling demands within expanded functions requires an active participation in instruction and planning. The tasks and leadership position advocated in this book require that library media specialists be highly-competent, assertive information professionals. And if these first two trends progress as indicated, the conflict in perceptions should be resolved. Success in meeting increased responsibilities and demands results in a positive self-image and recognition by others.

Throughout this book, an active, central role for the library media program in the overall educational program has been promoted. The importance of information-related support services to subject area curricula seems clear. In the near future, the library media center will increasingly act as the gateway from information (and information systems) to subject area curriculum. Equally vital is the role of the library media program in developing the skills associated with access, use, reformulation and evaluation of information.

In meeting the information needs of users, the library media program focuses on providing a full range of curriculum support services and teaching information problem-solving within a critical thinking skills context. In both cases, there is a professional responsibility to provide students with optimal learning environments in which to master life-long skills. In the future, one can envision the library media program at the center of content learning. The logical extension of successful skills instruction and support services functions is an active library media specialist totally involved in development of school curriculum.

As education becomes increasingly concerned with development of intellectual skills and processes (as opposed to focusing on content knowledge), the information problem-solving curriculum of the library media center moves to the core of overall educational goals and objectives. When library media specialists teach a library & information skills curriculum based on an information problem-solving strategy, they are teaching skills as basic as reading and arithmetic. The emphasis is on *process* and the overriding factor that determines the value of the library media center's instructional program is not the specific skills taught but the transferability of skills to situations across the curriculum.

The importance of information problem-solving skills in an information-oriented society is obvious. What should also be obvious is how these same skills link library media program objectives and subject area objectives. Educating students to be information-literate, able to locate, use, manipulate, present, and evaluate information effectively and efficiently to attain subject curriculum objectives, ties together the efforts of library media specialists and content area teachers. Both are indespensible if the overall curricular goals of the school are to be reached.

The changing orientation of the library media program from supplemental and enriching to central and basic increases the influence of the library media specialist within the educational environment. Acting in this capacity, the library media specialist is an equal partner with all other educators within the school in striving to attain overall school goals and objectives. Furthermore, as skills are best learned in the environment where they will be used, many of the activities of students will take place in library media centers and other information settings. In this way, the library media center serves as a physical as well as a conceptual center for curriculum.

The curriculum support services function also contributes to moving the library media program to the center of the educational process. Working with teachers and administrators to better utilize information in instructional settings, library media specialists increase their curriculum consultation and development activities. This results in:

- increased interaction among subject area faculty, administrators, and library media specialists;
- recognition by other school personnel of the viability and value of the library media program as a center for content learning;
- perceptions of the library media specialist as a knowledgeable, professional member of the educational team;
- significant increases in the variety and range of information systems used as sources of information by teachers and students;
- equally significant increases in the formats used by teachers and students to communicate and present knowledge and ideas; and
- pressure and demands on the administrative side of the library media program to be able to manage the logistics of a program at the center of the educational process.

In providing essential information-based curriculum support services, the library media center is participatory rather than reactionary. Few subject areas will be untouched by the library media center and the library media specialist. In essence, the library media center becomes a foundation for successful educational programming.

Within this vision, information concerns are a focal point in all important curriculum decisions. The library media specialist becomes the natural facilitator for content learning, the professional link between academic goals, information, and critical thinking skills. The result is a library media program at the center of content learning.

BEYOND THE SHORT-TERM

As library media programs have developed in schools, there has been a slow but noticeable change in the position of the library media program vís-a-vís the overall curriculum. Figures 12.1 through 12.5 graphically represent how library media programs are moving from an ancillary position to one at the center of the overall curricular program. This is an historical pattern, reflecting the growth of information needs of curriculum as well as changes in the more general educational environment. It is also a pattern being repeated today wherever professional library media specialists are creating new library media programs.

In its early form, the school library was little more than an add-on. It was independent and separate from the curriculum of the classroom (as represented in figure 12.1), and functioned primarily as a place for finding books for enrichment or personal enjoyment. As collections improved and the focus of library professionals changed to promoting reading and teaching skills for locating and accessing sources in the library, the school library was now in a position tangen-

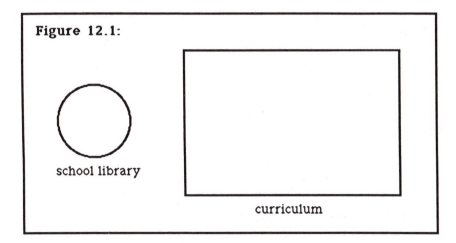

Figure 12.1.   Library Media Program/Curriculum Relationship: Phase 1

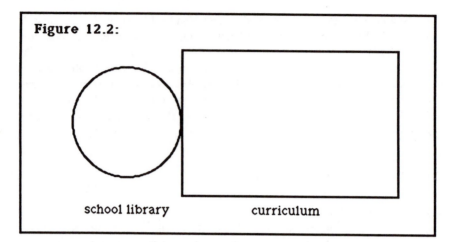

Figure 12.2.   Library Media Program/Curriculum Relationship: Phase 2

tial to the curriculum—still separate, but now more involved with educational concerns (see figure 12.2).

More recently, the crucial change in the school library program is the recognition of the relationship of the program to the curriculum. This is the general present-day situation of most school library media settings. There is an effort to focus on the requirements of the curriculum with a certain degree of overlap between library media services and the overall curriculum program (see figure 12.3). Unfortunately, this overlap is generally non-systematic, responsive in a

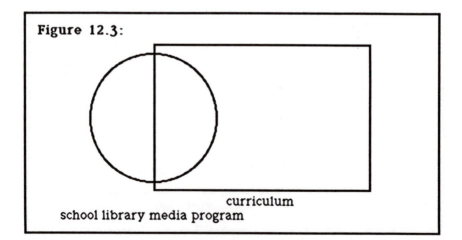

Figure 12.3.   Library Media Program/Curriculum Relationship: Phase 3

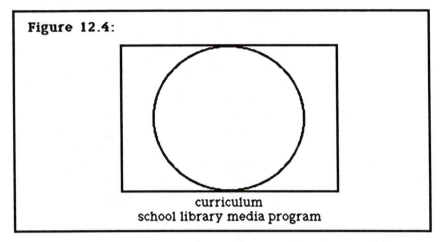

Figure 12.4.   **Library Media Program/Curriculum Relationship: Phase 4**

haphazard way to meeting curriculum demands. Some areas of the library media program remain outside the curriculum.

This book has been directed at developing a library media program totally congruent with the curriculum (see figure 12.4). This is the short-term future of the library media program as envisioned above. The curriculum support services and library & information skills functions exist completely in concert with the overall curriculum program of the school. Many library media programs are already seeking to bring about this situation. Adopting the Six Stage-Strategy and the Big Six Skills curriculum will move the process forward.

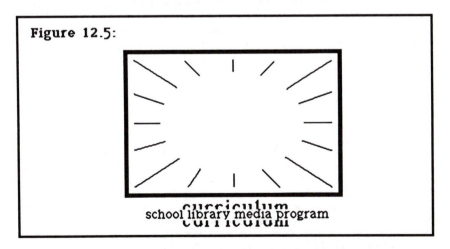

Figure 12.5.   **Library Media Program/Curriculum Relationship: Phase 5**

Ultimately, the library media program must pervade the entire curriculum. In the long-term, the likely "explosion" of library media functions makes it impossible to talk about library media issues as separate from those of the overall educational program (figure 12.5). Today, the library media program is concerned with skills instruction and information-based curriculum. Tomorrow, these are the overriding concerns of education. Information support services for curriculum become crucial to the day-to-day business of education. Information problem-solving, emphasized, reinforced, and used in every area of curriculum, is viewed as a basic skill taught along with reading, writing, and computation.

This view of the centrality of information-related support services and instruction in information problem-solving skills is entirely consistent with predictions about future trends in education.* Most speculations on the future of education include these common predictions:

- a decentralized educational system;
- the availability and encouragement of lifelong learning;
- a heavy reliance on communication and computer technology; and
- an emphasis on developing the problem-solving, analytical, and other high-level cognitive skills, necessary for living in an information age.

Clarke, for example, describes a futuristic educational environment markedly different from that found in today's schools:

On the evening of July 20, 2019, John Stanton is taking yet another teleclass. His classroom is actually a room in his home outfitted for teleconferencing. At the moment he is posing a question to his teacher. Sitting in a university video studio 1,400 miles away, the teacher appears in the room as a life-size three-dimensional holographic image. . . .

Across town at a McSchool franchise, a grandmother is taking a course in small-business management. Two rooms away her 16-year-old grandson is getting first-year college English out of the way early. (Clarke, Arthur C. *July 20, 2019: Life in the 21st Century*, 1986, p. 75)

Clarke further states that,

---

* Most authors speculating on the future include sections about education. Readers interested in general works are referred to Alvin Toffler's *The Third Wave* (New York: Morrow, 1980), John Naisbitt's *Megatrends* (New York: Warner Books, 1982), and Arthur C. Clarke's *July 20, 2019: Life in the 21st Century* (New York: Macmillan, 1986). Two government works specifically focusing on education are: *Information Technology and Its Impact on American Education* (U.S. Congress, Office of Technology Assessment, Washington, D.C.: Government Printing Office, 1982) and *A Nation at Risk* (National Committee on Excellence in Education, Washington, D.C.: Government Printing Office, 1983). Finally Liesener's "Learning at Risk: School Library Media Programs in an Information World," *School Library Media Quarterly*, Fall 1985 offers a future orientation from the library media perspective.

In [the] new computer-based economy, more and more jobs will involve the creation, transmission and processing of information and ideas. As the number of jobs based on muscle and mindless repetition wanes, industry and business will increasingly require workers with sharp thinking skills. And, because most people will be taking courses lifelong, they will need to know how to learn—education itself will be a skill that virtually everyone will need. As a result, the emphasis in elementary and high school will shift: In the school of the future the focus will be on teaching how to think and how to learn. (Clarke, p. 76)

While not as fanciful as Clarke's descriptions, The U.S. Congress Office of Technology Assessment reports strikingly similar conclusions about the direction of education in the United States:

1. The so-called information revolution, driven by rapid advances in communication and computer technology, is profoundly affecting American education. It is changing the nature of what needs to be learned, who needs to learn it, who will provide it, and how it will be provided and paid for.

2. Information technology can potentially improve and enrich the educational services that traditional educational institutions provide, distribute education and training into new environments such as the home and office, reach new clients such as handicapped or homebound persons, and teach job-related skills in the use of technology. Informational Technology and Its Impact on American Education. Washington, D.C.: Government Printing Office, 1983, p. iii)

These and other similar works point to an educational system highly-dependent on information and highly-involved with developing information-related skills. The extensive use of alternative media, information, and communication systems for delivery of instruction and the focus on skills required for life in an information age are the central concerns of both the library media program and the overall educational program. In fact, it is difficult to imagine any aspect of the educational program not integrally involved with information-related skills and services.

While the validity of library media program concerns in the educational system of the future seems firmly established, the actual role of library media specialists may be less clear. A future as described above requires that all educators be involved in information-related activities to some degree. When information problem-solving is as basic as reading, writing, and arithmetic, all teachers must be knowledgeable and able to use, teach, and reinforce information problem-solving skills. Similarly, all educators will need to be able to (1) collect, use, synthesize and evaluate information from a myriad of information systems, and (2) deliver instruction using different media formats and communication systems. What then is the role of the library media specialist in an educational system where everyone has a high degree of competence in information areas?

In current positions, library media professionals are actually more generalists than specialists. Today's library media professional must be flexible and able to deliver a wide range of curriculum support and instructional services to the total educational community. In the long-term, one possible direction is a movement toward specialization by library media personnel. While still sharing a common core of knowledge, competencies and abilities, library & information specialists may be required to choose particular areas of specialization. Working under the umbrella of a broad library & information center, these specializations may relate to current library media concerns (e.g. curriculum development, reading guidance, information service, administration, media production) or involve new areas (e.g. telecommunications systems design, information systems management, and information delivery).

There will also be important roles to play in working with educators in professional development and consultation. Someone must be available to advise and train teachers, administrators and support staff in applying information-based approaches to curriculum and instruction. To act in this capacity, library & information specialists must be skilled in using information technology and systems as well have a clear vision of how information and technology are to be used in education. In fulfilling this role, library & information specialists provide expert assistance to educators.

Finally, there are always key persons who provide direction and work to reshape education. The professionals responsible for overall coordination of library media services—the library & information program managers—must offer leadership in the effort to determine educational purpose and formulate, state and achieve goals in an information-centered environment. In addition to providing overall coordination and management of the library & information program, these high-level managers are the leaders who link the information society to education.

Obviously we are a long way from this vision of the future. At each step along the way there are exciting and significant opportunities for library media professionals. We challenge you to rise to the opportunities and offer the perspectives, concepts, and strategies of this book as you look to the future.

APPENDIX A: TYPES OF SOURCES/SYSTEMS TO BE CONSIDERED UNDER LOCATION & ACCESS SKILLS

1. General Organization of the Library Media Center
2. Catalog
   manual
   online
3. General Reference Materials
   almanacs
   current event sources
   dictionaries
   encyclopedias
   government statistical sources
   indexes to magazines
   indexes to newspapers
   maps, globes, atlas, graphs, gazateers
   resource (vertical) file
   special dictionaries
   thesauri
   yearbooks and annuals
4. Beyond the Library Media Center
   interlibrary loan
   library media networks
   OCLC/RLIN
   public and university connections
5. Subject-Specific Reference Materials
   Arts & Humanities
   Biography
   Business
   Careers & Occupation
   Colleges & University Sources
   Foreign Languages
   Geography

Health & Safety
History/Chronology
Home Economics
Literature & Literary Criticism
Mathematics
Politics & Government
Sciences
Social Sciences
Sports & Physical Education
Technology

Note: Materials in the above categories will likely include traditional book and serial formats as well as new microform, computer-based, and multimedia ones.

Appendix B: Time Management Study*

This appendix outlines the steps required for conducting a time management study. The purpose of a time management study is to determine the time spent by an individual on various tasks. The procedure may be implemented by an independent outside observer or as a self-analysis.

A time management study is a useful research technique for documenting how much time library media specialists and others spend on various functions. It is particularly valuable for gathering data to test the accuracy of preconceptions about how time is (or should be) spent. Within the Six-Stage Strategy, the results of a time management study are useful for resource feasibility analysis, planning, and documenting needs to administrators.

As a procedure based on sampling, the time management study should be carried out over a series of days and at various times during the year. There is a certain amount of error of estimate in any sampling procedure. Error is minimized by sampling more days from the total number of work days and randomizing the selection of days for study. In order to present a reliable picture and lessen potential biasing effects, a complete time management study is best conducted over an entire school year.

For example, for a school situation in which library media specialists work approximately 180 days, a recommended minimal sample is 20 days (slightly over 10% of the total days). To further minimize bias the 20 days should be divided equally by the days of the week (i.e., 4 each), and equally divided across the 4 quarters of the school year (i.e., 5 days sampled in each quarter). As quarters usually contain 10 weeks, 1 day could be sampled every other week. Adjustments can be made for days off and special events, however care should be taken to make the selection of specific days as random as possible.

While a full-year study is recommended, more limited studies can be useful for gaining an idea of how time is spent in specific situations. If no information is available on how library media specialists or support staff spend their time, it is certainly reasonable to conduct a limited study (sampling, for example, 1 day a week over a 5 week period). However, in these limited studies, caution should be taken to resist the temptation to make overall conclusions and generalizations.

---

* This approach to time management is based on lectures by Evelyn Daniel.

STEPS IN CONDUCTING A TIME MANAGEMENT STUDY

I. Planning

1. Determine the person or person(s) to study.
2. Determine whether the study will be a self-study or done by an outside observer.
3. Determine the number of days to be sampled and the specific dates.
4. Set up the categories for the worksheet (see column headings in figure B.1).

The categories listed should be based upon the objectives of the study. For example, figure B.1 includes the general library media functions of information service, consultation, administration, instruction, and technical services. An "other" category is necessary to allow for breaks, lunch, and other personal time. The intent here is to determine the relative time allotted to various professional tasks vs. technical (nonprofessional) tasks. Headings could easily be expanded to include other functions important to study (e.g. reading guidance, media production, and/or curriculum development).

5. Set up the time blocks for the worksheet. From the beginning of the day to the end, divide up into equal blocks. (In the example, the day begins at 8:00, ends at 3:00 and is divided into 15 minute blocks). If the division breaks completely coincide with the period breaks of the school, offset the blocks by 5 min. (i.e., if all periods start on the hour, and end at :55, offset to :05, :20, :35, :50).
6. Prepare all worksheets that will be needed.

II. Data Collection

7. Beginning with the first time listed (8:00 in figure B.1), check the box that best describes the activity that you are doing. You can select one category per time break.
8. During the day, pause at each time break and again check the box that best describes what you are doing. Accuracy is essential. You are to check the most appropriate category for the activity that you are actually engaged in—not what you would like to be doing, what you should be doing, or what you wish you were doing. The category checked should be the best description of what you were actually doing.
9. If you forget a time break, reflect on what you were doing at that time and check the appropriate box. Again try to document exactly what it is you were doing. Try to avoid having to make retrospective judgments. After a

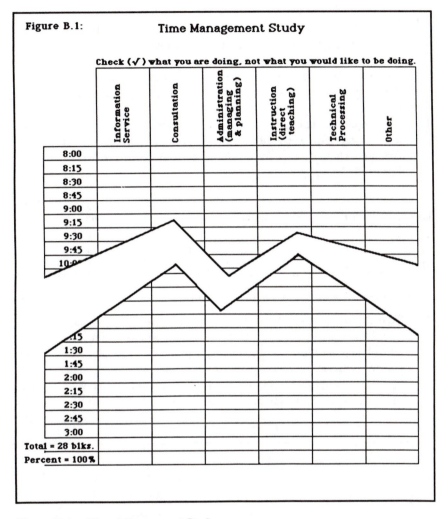

Figure B.1.   Time Management Study

while most persons become accustomed to pausing briefly every 15 min or
so.

10.   Try not to think about prior checkmarks or any pattern. Sampling in this
way, over time, will average out any specific checkmark and give a reasonably accurate picture of general trends.

11.   Breaks, lunch, and personal time are all legitimate parts of one's day and
must be noted in the "other" column.

III. Data Analysis

12. Results should be tallied and analyzed after the complete study is finished. To tally after each day may bias the study.
13. To tally a given sheet, add up the subtotal for each column then add across the columns to confirm against the grand total of possible checks (in the example, 28).
14. To compile and tally total data, create a separate sheet listing each day and the subtotals associated with each function. Then add up the totals for each function. These data are the raw frequencies associated with each function. For example,

DAY	isv	con	adm	inst	tec	oth	TOTAL
day 1	2	1	8	0	9	8	28
day 2	4	2	6	0	10	6	28
day 3	4	1	9	1	8	5	28
TOTALS	10	4	23	1	27	19	84

15. To determine percent of time spent in each function for each day divide the raw frequencies by the total of all possible checkmarks for that day (e.g. 28 above) and multiply by 100. To determine average percents for each category, divide the column totals by the grand total of the study (e.g. 84 above) and multiply by 100 (the percents in the example below are rounded off to the nearest integer and thus do not always total to exactly 100). For example:

DAY	isv	con	adm	inst	tec	oth
day 1	7%	4%	29%	0%	32%	29%
day 2	14%	7%	21%	0%	36%	21%
day 3	14%	4%	32%	4%	29%	18%
AVG. PERCENT	12%	5%	27%	1%	32%	23%

16. To be more complete in reviewing and presenting results, it is useful to consider the average percent in a function along with the low to high range. In the example above, technical services can be described as averaging approximately 32% of the person's time, ranging from 29% to 32% on any given day. In comparison to a common preconception, this figure would be considered appropriate for a clerical staff person but not for a library media specialist.
17. Additional summary statistics (e.g. standard deviation, standard error of estimate, median) may be computed and presented as desired, however for most situations, percents with ranges are generally adequate.

BIBLIOGRAPHY

In addition to works cited in this book, this bibliography contains resources that school library media specialists should find particularly helpful when addressing curriculum concerns.

"Alliance for Excellence," *School Library Journal* 31, no. 1, (September 1984): 11.

American Association of School Librarians. *Standards for School Library Programs.* Chicago: American Library Association, 1960.

American Association of School Librarians and the Association for Educational Communications and Technology. *Media Programs: District and School.* Chicago: American Library Association, 1975.

American Association of School Librarians and the Department of Audiovisual Instruction of the National Education Association. *Standards for School Media Programs.* Chicago: American Library Association, 1969.

Baker, D. Philip. *The Library Media Program and the School.* Littleton, CO: Libraries Unlimited, 1984.

Barron, Daniel D. "Communicating What SLM Specialists Do: The Evaluation Process." *School Library Journal* 33, no. 6 (March 1987): 95–99.

Berkowitz, Bob and Berkowitz, Joyce. "Thinking is Critical: Moving Students Beyond Location." *School Library Media Activities Monthly* 3, no. 9 (May 1987): 26–27.

Bertland, Linda H. "An Overview of Research in Metacognition: Implications for Informations Skills Instruction." In "Current Research," *School Library Media Quarterly* 14, no. 2, (Winter 1986): 96–99.

Bloom, Benjamin S., et al., *Taxonomy of Educational Objectives: The Classification of Educational Goals: Handbook I: Cognitive Domain.* New York: McKay, 1956.

Bondy, Elizabeth. "Thinking about Thinking." *Childhood Education* 60, no. 4 (March/April 1984): 234–238.

Callison, Daniel. "School Library Media Programs and Free Inquiry Learning." *School Library Journal* 33, no. 5 (February 1986): 20.

Carlson, Eric D. "Decision Support Systems: Personal Computing Services for Managers." *Management Review* 66, no. 1 (January 1977): 4–11.

Chisholm, Margaret E. and Ely, Donald P. *Media Personnel in Education.* Englewood Cliffs, NJ: Prentice-Hall, 1976.

Chisholm, Margaret E. and Ely, Donald P. *Instructional Design and the Library Media Specialist.* Chicago: American Library Association, 1979.

Churchman, C. West. *The Systems Approach.* NY: Dell Publishing Co., Inc., 1968.

Clarke, Arthur C. *July 20, 2019: Life in the 21st Century.* NY: MacMillan Publishing Co., 1986.

Cleaver, Betty P. *Involving the School Library Media Specialist in Curriculum Development.* Chicago: American Association of School Librarians, American Library Association, 1983.

Conant, A. N. *The Conant Report: A Study of the Education of Librarians.* Cambridge, MA: The MIT Press, 1980.

Cook, Beth and Truett, Carol. "Media Specialists and Microcomputers: 13 Aspects of a Changing Role." *Media and Methods* 21, no. 4 (December 1984): 26, 31–33.

Costa, Betty and Costa, Marie. *A Micro Handbook,* 2nd ed. Littleton, CO: Libraries Unlimited, 1986.

Craver, Kathleen W. "The Changing Instructional Role of the High School Library Media Specialist: 1950–84." *School Library Media Quarterly* 14, no. 4 (Summer 1986): 183–191.

Davies, Ruth Ann. *The School Library Media Program,* 3rd ed. New York: Bowker, 1979.

Diehl, Carol et al. *A Response to Reports Seeking School Excellence from a School Library Media Perspective.* Madison, WI: Council on Library and Network Development of the Wisconsin Department of Public Instruction, 1984. (ED 245 684).

Eisenberg, Michael, "Changing Roles of the Media Specialist," ERIC Digest, Syracuse, New York: ERIC Clearinghouse on Information Resources, 1987.

Eisenberg, Michael. "Curriculum Mapping and Implementation of an Elementary School Library Media Skills Curriculum." *School Library Media Quarterly* 12, no. 2 (Fall 1984): 411–418.

Eisenberg, Michael and Notowitz, Carol I. "Booktalks: Creating Contagious Enthusiasm." *Media & Methods* 15, no. 7 (March 1979): 32–33.

Eisenberg, Michael and Notowitz, Carol I. "Managing the Library and Information Skills Program: Developing Support Systems for Planning and Implementation." *School Library Media Activities Monthly* II, no. 7 (March 1986): 27–33.

Elementary Library Media Skills Curriculum. Albany, NY: Bureau of School Libraries, New York State Education Department, 1980.

Elkind, David. *Child Development in Education: A Piagetian Perspective.* Oxford University Press, 1976.

Ely, Donald P. "The Role of the School Media Specialist: Some Directions and Choices," *Journal of Research and Development and Education* 16, no. 1 (November 1, 1982): 33–36.

English, Fenwick W. "Curriculum Development Within the School System." In: *Considered Action for Curriculum Development,* edited by Arthur W. Fishay, 149. Alexandria, VA: American Association of School Admnistrators, 1980.

English, Fenwick W. *Quality Control in Curriculum Development.* Alexandria, VA: American Association of School Administrators, 1978.

English, Fenwick W. "Re-tooling Curriculum with On-going School Systems." *Educational Technology,* (May 1979): 8–9.

Ennis, Robert. "A Concept of Critical Thinking." *Harvard Educational Review* 32, no. 1 (Winter 1962): 81–111.

Ericson, LaVaugh S. and Carmody, Jean. "Integrating Library Skills With Instruction." *Wilson Library Bulletin,* (January–February 1971): 23–26.

Fayol, Henri. *General and Industrial Management.* Revised ed. NY: Institute of Electrical and Electronics Engineers, 1984.

Flavell, J. H. *Cognitive Development.* Englewood Cliffs, N.J.: Prentice-Hall, 1977.

Gerlach, Vernon and Ely, Donald. *Teaching and Media: A Systematic Approach,* 2nd ed. Englewood Cliffs, NJ: Prentice-Hall, 1980.

Gustafson, Kent L. and Smith, Jane Bandy. *Research for School Media Specialists.* Georgia: University of Georgia. Department of Educational Media and Librarianship, 1982.

Hale, Robert G. and Others. *A Guide to School Library Media Programs.* Hartford, CT: Connecticut State Board of Education, 1982 (ED230 201).

Hart, Thomas L., ed. *Instruction in School Library Media Center Use*. Chicago: American Library Association, 1985.

Haycock, Carl Ann. "Information Skills in the Curriculum: Developing a School-Based Continuum." *Emergency Librarian*, (Sept./Oct. 1985): 11–17.

Hortin, John A. "The Changing Role of the School Media Specialist." *TechTrends* 30, no. 6 (September 1985): 20–21.

Hughes, Carolyn S. "Teaching Strategies for Developing Student Thinking: Strategies for Teachers and for Library Media Sepcialists." *School Library Media Quarterly* 15, no. 1 (Fall 1986): 33–36.

Informational Technology and Its Impact on American Education. Office of Technological Assessment. U.S. Congresses. Washington, D.C. (April 1983).

"Integrating Library Skills into Content Areas: Sample Units and Lesson Planning Forms." Honolulu: Hawaii State Department of Education. (November 1979) (ED 198 833).

Jay, Hilda L. *Stimulating Student Search: Library media / classroom teacher techniques*. Hamden, CT: Library Professional Publications; Shoe String Press, 1983.

Jay, M. Ellen. "The Elementary School Library Media Teacher's Role in Educating Students to Think Suggested Activities for Fostering the Development of Thinking Skills." *School Library Media Quarterly* 15, no. 1 (Fall 1986): 28–32.

Jay, M. Ellen, and Jay, Hilda L. *Building Reference Skills in the Elementary School*. Library Professional Publications; Shoe String Press, 1986.

Koberg, Don, and Bagnall, Jim. *The Universal Traveler, A Soft-Systems Guide to Creativity, Problem-Solving and the Process of Reaching Goals*. Los Altos, California: William Kaufmann, 1980.

Kuhlthau, Carol Collier. "A Process Approach to Library Skills Instruction." *School Library Media Quarterly* 13, no. 1 (Winter 1985a): 35–40.

Kuhlthau, Carol Collier. "Finding Meaning in Library media Centers." *School Library Media Activties Monthly* 1, no. 8 (April 1985b): 30–31.

Kuhlthau, Carol Collier. *Teaching The Library Research Process: A Step-by-Step Program for Secondary School Students*. West Nyack, NY: Center for Applied Research in Education, 1985c.

Liesener, James W. *Learning at Risk: School Library Media Programs in an Information World*. Office of Educational Research and Improvement, Center for Libraries and Education Improvement, Washington, DC, 1984. (ED 243 889). In *School Library Media Quarterly* 13, no. 1 (Fall, 1985).

Liesener, James W. *A Systematic Process for Planning Media Programs*. Chicago: American Library Association, 1976.

Library Skills Curriculum Activities/Objectives, K–12. Maine Educational Media Association, 1984 (ED 252 222).

Loertscher, David. "The Second Revolution: A Taxonomy for the 1980's." *Wilson Library Bulletin* 56, no. 6 (February 1982): 417–21.

McTighe, Jay and Schollenberger, Jan. "Why Teach Thinking: a Statement of Rationale", *Developing Minds: A Resource Book for Teaching Thinking*, edited by Arthur L. Costa. Alexandria, VA: Association for Supervision and Curriculum Development, 1985.

Mager, Robert F. *Preparing Instructional Objectives*. Palo Alto, California: Fearon Publishers, 1962.

Mancall, Jacqueline C., Aaron, Shirley L. and Walker, Sue A. "Educating Students to

Think: The Role of the School Library Media Program." *School Library Media Quarterly* 15, no. 1 (Fall 1986): 18–27.

Markuson, Carolyn. "Making It Happen: Taking Charge of the Information Curriculum.." *School Library Media Quarterly* 15, no. 1 (Fall 1986): pp. 37–40. (EJ 344 242).

A Nation at Risk: The Imperative for Educational Reform. National Commission on Exellence in Education. U.S. Department of Education. Washington, D.C.: U.S. Government Printing Office, April, 1983.

New Part 100 of the Commissioner's Regulations. Albany, NY: New York State Education Department, November, 1984.

Naisbett, John. *Megatrends: Ten New Directions Transforming Our Lives.* NY; Warner Books, Inc., 1982.

Piaget, J. *The Origins of Intelligence in Children.* New York: International Universities Press, 1952.

Prostano, Emanual T. and Prostano, Joyce S. *The School Library Media Center,* 3rd ed. Littleton, CO: Libraries Unlimited, 1982.

Sanders, Norris M. *Classroom Questions: What Kinds?* New York: Harper and Row, 1966.

Secondary Library Media and Information Skills Syllabus: Grades 7–12. Albany, NY: Bureau of School Library Media Programs and Bureau of Curriculum Development New York State Education Department, 1986. (draft)

Shapiro, Lillian L. *Serving Youth.* New York: Bowker, 1975.

Sprague, Ralph H. "A Framework for the Development of Decision Support Systems." *Information Systems Quarterly* (December 1980): 1–24.

Study Skills Related to Library Use: A K–12 Curriculum Guide for Teachers and Librarians. Honolulu, Hawaii: Hawaii State Department of Education, 1978. (ED 231 386).

Sullivan, Peggy. "Performance Standards for SLM Centers: Taking the Initiative." *School Library Journal* 32, no. 9 (May 1986): 48–49.

Teacher Handbook: Library/Media and Computer Skills Grades –12: North Carolina Competency-Based Curriculum. Raleigh, NC: Division of School Media Programs, Division of Computer Services, Media and Technology Services in cooperation with Instructional Services, North Carolina Department of Public Instruction, 1985.

Thompson, Loren C. and Frager, Alan M. "Teaching Critical Thinking: Guideline for Teacher-Designed Content Area Lessons." *Journal of Reading* 28 (November 1984): 122–127.

Toffler, Alvin. *The Third Wave.* New York: Morrow, 1980.

Troutner, Joanne. *The Media Specialist, the Microcomputer, and the Curriculum.* Littleton, CO: Libraries Unlimited, 1983.

Turner, Philip M. *Helping Teachers Teach.* Littleton, CO: Libraries Unlimited, 1985.

Walker, H. Thomas and Montgomery, Paula. *Teaching Library Media Skills.* 2nd ed. Littleton, CO: Libraries Unlimited, 1983.

Wehmeyer, Lillian D. *The School Librarian as Educator.* 2nd ed. Littleton, CO: Libraries Unlimited, 1984.

White, Howard D. and Calhoun, Karen. "Mapping a Curriculum by Computer," *Journal of the American Society for Information Science* 35, no. 2 (March 1984): 82–89.

Woolls, E. Blanche and Loertscher, David V., eds. *The Microcomputer Facility and the School Library Media Specialist.* Chicago: American Library Association, 1986.

Author Index

A

Aaron, S.L., 9, *169*

B

Bagnall, J., 20, *169*
Baker, D.P., *167*
Barron, D.D., *167*
Berkowitz, B., 106, *167*
Berkowitz, J., *167*
Bertland, L.H., *167*
Bloom, B.S., 37, 99, 101, *167*
Bondy, E., *167*

C

Calhoun, K., *170*
Callison, D., *167*
Carlson, E.D., 23, *167*
Carmody, J., *168*
Chisholm, M.E., 9, 12, *167*
Churchman, C.W., *167*
Clarke, A.C., 158, 159, *167*
Cleaver, B.P., *167*
Conant, A.N., 11, *167*
Cook, B., 13, *167*
Costa, B., 13, *168*
Costa, M., 13, *168*
Craver, 9

D

Davies, R.A., 9, *168*
Diehl, C., 14, *168*

E

Eisenberg, M., 37, 71, 73, 91, 106, *168*
Elkind, D., *168*
Ely, D.P., 9, 11, 12, 14, *167, 168*
English, F.W., 37, 71, 72, 73, 74, *168*
Ennis, R., 101, *168*
Ericson, L.S., *168*

F

Fayol, H., *168*
Flavell, J.H., *168*
Frager, A.M., *170*

G

Gerlach, V., 12, *168*
Gustafson, K.L., *168*

H

Hale, R.G., *168*
Hart, T.L., *169*
Haycock, C.A., *169*
Hortin, J.A., 9, 11, *169*
Hughes, C.S., *169*

J

Jay, H.L., *169*
Jay, M.E., *169*

K

Koberg, D., 20, *169*
Kuhlthau, C.C., 100, 101, *169*

L

Liesener, J.W., 14, 18, 49, 88, *169*
Loertscher, D.V., 13, *169, 170*

M

Mager, R.F., *169*
Mancall, J.C., 9, *169*
Markuson, C., *170*
McTighe, J., *169*
Montgomery, P., 37, *170*

N

Naisbett, J., *170*
Notowitz, C.I., 91, *168*

P
Piaget, J., 101, *170*
Prostano, E.T., 9, 18, 49, *170*
Prostano, J.S., 9, 18, 39, *170*

S
Sanders, N.M., *170*
Schollenberger, J., *169*
Shapiro, L., 9, *170*
Smith, J.B., *168*
Sprague, R.H., 23, *170*
Sullivan, P., *170*

T
Toffler, A., *170*
Thompson, L.C., *170*
Troutner, J., *170*
Truett, C., 13, *167*
Turner, P.M., *170*

W
Walker, H.T., 9, 37, *170*
Walker, S.A., *169*
Wehmeyer, L.D., 37, *170*
White, H.D., *170*
Woolls, E.B., 13, *170*

Subject Index

Compiled by Larry Greenberg

A

Action, 7–8
Active role of library media specialist, 4, 10–11, 89, 153
Active thinking vocabulary, 103, 104
Agenda, 7
Appleworks, 76–77, 78
Approach of library media specialist, 7
Attitude of library media specialist, 7, 98
Audiovisual technologies, 89

B

Bagnall, Jim, 20
Berkowitz and Berkowitz, 103–104
Big Six Skills Curriculum, 37–38, 99–119, 150. *see also* Library & information skills curriculum
  and Bloom's taxonomy, 105
  computer use and, 105
  enroute objectives, 106
  evaluation (skill six), 101, 118–119
  general goal of, 108
  information seeking strategies (skill two), 101, 110–111
  in information support systems, 38–39
  integration with curriculum units, 57–60, 123
  introduced, 5, 37–38
  and library research process model, 100–101
  location and access to information (skill three), 101, 112–113, 161–162
  media use and, 105
  overview of, 101
  reading guidance and, 105
  scope and sequence of, 104, 106–119
  skills-by-unit matrix, 57–60
  synthesis (skill five), 101, 116–117
  task definition (skill one), 101, 108–109
  terminal objectives, 106
  top-down approach of, 20, 100
  use of information (skill four), 101, 114–115

Bloom, Benjamin S., 99–100, 101–104
Bloom's taxonomy of cognitive objectives, 99–100, 101–104
  active thinking vocabulary, 103, 104
  analysis level, 102
  application level, 102
  and Big Six Skills curriculum, 105
  comprehension level, 102
  evaluation level, 102
  and information oriented actions, 102
  knowledge level, 101–102
  and library & information skills curriculum, 103–104
  questions linked to, 103
  synthesis level, 102
Booktalks, 91
Building level
  curriculum councils, 95
  curriculum guides, 72
  information, 35–36
  planning groups, 34, 67, 122

C

Clarke, Arthur C., 158–159
Classroom content, *see* Classroom curriculum
Classroom curriculum, 5, 38, 72, 104. *see also* Curriculum units
Classroom instruction, *see* Classroom curriculum; Curriculum units
Cognitive behaviors, *see* Bloom's taxonomy of cognitive objectives
Cognitive levels, *see* Bloom's taxonomy of cognitive objectives
Cognitive objectives, *see* Bloom's taxonomy of cognitive objectives
Collection management role of library media specialist, 11. *see also* Resources provision
Community resources, 89
  file, 93, 94
Competencies of library media specialist, 3, 12, 88, 89, 96, 160

Comprehensive planning, 18–19, 49, 52–53.
see also Planning processes; Rolling
five-year plans
Computer
based economy, 158–159
involvement, 13, 89, 105
literacy, 13, 105
technologies, 13, 159
Conant study, 11
Content analysis, 73. see also Curriculum
maps and mapping
Content area curriculum units, see Curriculum
units
Content-based learning, 149, 155
Controlled vocabulary for curriculum database,
77
Cooperation as a resource, 50
Council on Library and Network Development
of the Wisconsin Department of Public
Instruction, 14
Craver, Kathleen W., 9, 10–11, 13
Critical thinking skills, 100, 102, 106. see also
Big Six Skills curriculum; Bloom's taxonomy of cognitive objectives
Curriculum
councils, 95
definition of, 3
concerns of library media program, 3–12,
31–33, 149–153
fictional curriculum, 37, 72
Curriculum consultation role of library specialist, 12, 62, 94–96, 152
services checklist, 95
Curriculum database, 36–37, 76–85. see also
Curriculum maps and mapping
controlled vocabulary for, 77
data entry, 77
data presentation (reports), 80–82, 84
defining the, 77–80
fields for, 74, 77–80
adapted for planning information, 63–64
reports, 80–82, 84
Curriculum decision making, see Curriculum
consultation; Curriculum development
Curriculum design, see Curriculum
development
Curriculum development, 96–98, 151, 152. see
also Curriculum maps and mapping;
Unit plans; Lesson plans
process for, 122–124
services, 61–62, 151, 152
services checklist, 97

Curriculum guides, 11, 36–37, 71–72
district or building level, 72
global or state, 72
library & information skills, 37
Curriculum information, 36–37, 71–72. see
also Curriculum guides; Curriculum
maps and mapping; Curriculum units
Curriculum maps and mapping, 71–85
curriculum support services perspective of,
45–46, 83–84
database, 36–37, 63, 76–85
data collection, 73–76
data evaluation, 83–84
data presentation (reports), 80–82, 84
data storage, 76–80
defined, 73
elementary school, 79, 80, 81
evaluation of, 83–84
fields of interest for, 74
holistic perspective of, 84
information sources for, 36–37, 71–72
introduced, 4, 37
library & information skills instruction perspective of, 45, 83–84
adapted for planning information, 63–64
reports, 80–82, 84
secondary school, 82
worksheet for, 75
Curriculum support activities, see Curriculum
support services
Curriculum support services, 4–5, 87–98, 150,
152
checklist, 39–40
curriculum consultation, 12, 62, 94–96,
152
services checklist, 95
curriculum development, 61–62, 96–98,
151, 152
services checklist, 97
and curriculum maps, 45–46, 83–84
evaluation of, 66–67
examples of, 40
and feasibility analysis, 45–47
future direction of, 98, 154–155
information service, 92–94, 151–152
services checklist, 93
introduced, 5, 27, 39–40
reading guidance, 11, 90–92, 150–151, 152
services checklist, 92
resources provision, 88–90, 152, 161–162
services checklist, 90
support services-by-unit matrix, 60–62

Curriculum units, 73
  and Big Six Skills, 57–60, 123
  and curriculum mapping, 73–84
  and curriculum support services, 45–46
  integration with library & information skills
    instruction, 45–47, 54–60, 83–84, 122–
    123
  introduced, 36, 73
  schedule of, 54–57, 124
  sequence of, 54
  skills-by-unit matrix, 57–60, 123
  subject area objectives of, 122
  support services-by-unit matrix, 60–62
  time frame for, 54

D
Daniel, Evelyn, 19
Data analysis for time management study, 166
Databases
  controlled vocabulary for, 77
  curriculum, 36–37, 63–64, 76–85
  database management programs, 76, 84
  data entry, 77
  data presentation, 80–82, 84
  defining, 77–80
  ERIC, 93
  fields for, 74, 77–80
  information, 94
  organizational information, 17, 94
  planning information, 63
  reports, 80–82, 84
Database management programs for curriculum
  mapping, 76, 84
Data collection
  for curriculum mapping, 73–76
    worksheet for, 75
  for time management study, 164–165
    worksheet for, 165
Data entry for curriculum mapping, 77
Data presentation for curriculum mapping, 80–
  82, 84
Data storage for curriculum mapping, 76–80
Dbase, 76–77
Decentralized education, 149, 158
Decision support systems, see also Support
  systems, 23–24, 33–41
Define goals and objectives (Six-Stage Strat-
  egy), 18, 30–32
Direct information service, see Information
  service
District
  curriculum councils, 95
  curriculum guides, 72
  planning group, 34
District and school goals and objectives, 3–4
Divergent thinking, 102. see also Big Six
  Skills curriculum; Bloom's taxonomy
  of cognitive objectives
DSS, see Decision support systems

E
Education
  contexts in, 16
  decentralized, 149, 158
  future of, 149, 153–160
  information based, 5, 38, 149
  systems in, 16
Eisenberg, Michael B., 37, 71, 73
Elementary school
  curriculum map, 79, 80, 81
  lesson plans, 136–138
  schedule of curriculum units, 55
  skills-by-unit matrix, 58
  support services-by-unit matrix, 61
  unit plans, 131–135
  year schedule, 64
Ely, Donald, 11, 12, 14
English, Fenwick W., 37, 71, 72, 73, 74
Enroute objectives of Big Six Skills curriculum, 106
Equipment, see Resources provision
ERIC (Educational Resources Information
  Center), 93
Evaluation (Big Six Skills), 101, 118–119
Evaluation of plans and processes (Six-Stage
  Strategy), 65–68
  curriculum maps, 83–84
  curriculum support services, 66–67
  five-year plans, 65–66
  in problem-solving model, 22
  lesson plans, 67
  library & information skills curriculum, 66
  one-year plans, 66–67
  plans, 65
  Six-Stage Strategy, 68
  unit plans, 67
Expanded role of library media specialist, 11–
  13, 153

F
Facilities, see Resources provision
Fayol, Henri, 18

Feasibility analysis (Six-Stage Strategy), 43–50, 122
  program, 43, 44–47
    of curriculum support services, 45–47
    of integration of library & information skills instruction and classroom curriculum, 45–47
    priority setting for, 46–47
  resources, 47–50
    available resources, 47, 49
    cooperation, 50
    priority setting for, 50
    time, professional and support staff, 47–49
  time management study, 163–166
Fictional curriculum, 37, 72
Fields of interest for curriculum mapping, 74
Five-year plans, 19, 49, 52–53. *see also* Rolling five-year plans
Format for lesson plans, *see* Lesson plans, format for
Format for unit plans, *see* Unit plans, format for
Future of library media program, 98, 140–160
  short-term, 149, 153–155
  long-term, 149, 155–160

G
Gantt chart, 54
Global curriculum guides, 72
Global program planning, *see* Comprehensive planning; Rolling five-year plans
Goals and objectives
  Big Six Skills curriculum, 106, 108
  defining (Six-Stage Strategy), 18, 30–32
  evaluation of, 65–68
  of five-year plans, 52–53
  goals, examples of, 31
  objectives, examples of, 31–32
  of one-year plans, 54
  in the problem-solving model, 22
  statement of, 32
  subject area objectives, 122
Group approach, *see* Planning groups
Guides, *see* Curriculum guides

H
High level managers, *see* Library & information program managers
Higher thinking skills, 102, 103–104. *see also* Big Six Skills curriculum; Bloom's taxonomy of cognitive objectives
Historical pattern of library media program, 155–157
Holistic perspective of curriculum maps, 84
Hortin, John A., 11
Human support systems, *see* Support systems, human

I
Information
  based education, 5, 38, 149
  building level, 35–36
  curriculum, 36–37, 71–72
  databases, 94
  files, 94
  literacy, 99, 154
  needs, 38, 151, 153
    of students, 38, 105, 151–152
  organizational, 17, 35–36, 94
  planning, 63–64
  technologies, 159
Information problem-solving process, 99–101, 105–107, 150. *see also* Big Six Skills curriculum
  in the future, 149, 153–154
  introduced, 5, 38
  and reading guidance, 105
  and students, 38–39, 150
  teachers use of, 159
  top-down approach to, 38–39, 100
Information seeking strategies (Big Six Skills), 101, 110–111
  worksheet for, 138
Information services, 92–94, 151–152
  checklist, 93
  and society, 151–152
Information support systems, *see* Support systems, information
Information systems, 151
Input-process-output model, 17
Inputs and outputs, 17–18, 43, 47
Instructional design role of library media specialist, 12. *see also* Curriculum development
Integrated skills instruction, *see* Integration of library & information skills instruction and classroom curriculum
Integrated units, *see* Integration of library & information skills instruction and classroom curriculum

Integration of library & information skills instruction and classroom curriculum, 5, 38, 45–47, 54–60, 83–84, 122–123, 151. *see also* Curriculum maps and mapping; library & information skills curriculum
Interdisciplinary curriculum units, 46. *see also* Curriculum units

K

Koberg, Don, 20
Kulthau, Carol Collier, 100–101

L

Lesson plans, 121–147. *see also* Unit plans
  developing, 122–124
  elementary school, 136–138
  evaluation of, 67
  format for, 127–129
  introduced, 19, 63–65
  secondary school, 145–147
  writing, 124
Libraries, 151
Library & information program managers, 160
Library & information skills instruction, *see* Big Six Skills curriculum; Library & information skills curriculum
Library & information skills instruction curriculum, 99–119, 150–151. *see also*, Big Six Skills curriculum; Unit plans; Lesson plans
  and Bloom's taxonomy, 103–104
  and curriculum development, 96
  evaluation of, 66
  and feasibility analysis, 44–45
  in information support systems, 37–39
  integration with classroom curriculum, 5, 38, 45–47, 54–60, 83–84, 122–123
  introduced, 5, 37–39
  adapting to local situation, 38–39
  and reading guidance, 105
  and Regent's Action Plan, 48–49
  skills-by-unit matrix, 57–60, 123
  top-down approach to, 20, 38–39
Library classes, 38
Library media center, 3, 5, 96, 154–155
Library media professional support groups, 34–35
Library media services, *see* Curriculum support services

Library media skills, *see* Library & information skills curriculum
Library media specialist
  action orientation of, 7–8
  agenda of, 7
  approach of, 7
  attitude of, 7, 98
  competencies of, 3, 12, 88, 89, 96, 160
  and computer involvement, 13, 89
  gaining respect, 50
  problems of, 6
  and professional support groups, 34–35
  role of
    active, 4, 10–11, 89, 153
    collection management, 11
    curriculum consultation, 12, 62, 94–96, 152
    curriculum development, 61–62, 96–98, 151, 152
    expanded, 11–13, 153
    future, 153–160
    information service, 92–94, 151–152
    instructional design, 12
    literature on, 9–11
    mediation, 14
    passive, 10, 89
    patterns and trends of, 10–11
    perceptions of, 11
    reading guidance, 11, 90–92, 150–151, 152
    redefined, 13–14
    resources provision, 88–90, 152
    teaching, 10, 12, 88
    traditional, 10
Library media support services, *see also* Curriculum support services
Library research process model, 100–101
Liesener, James W., 14, 18
Lifelong learning skills, 149, 158
Linear planning, 19–20
Literacy, promotion of, *see* Reading guidance
Literature appreciation, *see* Reading guidance
Literature, promotion of, *see* Reading guidance
Literature on the role of the library media specialist, 9–11
Local curriculum guides, *see* Curriculum guides, district
Local planning groups, 34, 67, 122
Location and access to information (Big Six Skills), 101, 112–113, 161–162
  sources and systems for, 161–162

Long-term planning, *see* Comprehensive planning; Rolling five-year plan

M

Management concepts and tools, *see* Planning processes
Management information systems, 23
Management processes, *see* Planning processes
Managers, 18
 library & information program managers, 160
Mapping information, *see* Curriculum maps and mapping
Materials provision, *see* Resources provision
Media use and the Big Six Skills, 105
Mediation function of library media specialist, 14
MIS, *see* Management Information System, 23
Mission statement, 3–4

N

New York State Education Department
 Regents Action Plan, 48–49
Nontext materials, 46, 89

O

Objectives, *see* Goals and objectives
One-year plans, 54–64, 66–67, 121
 alternative presentations of, 63–64
 use of curriculum database for, 63–64
 evaluation of, 66–67
 goals and objectives of, 54
 skills-by-unit matrix, 57–60, 123
 support services-by-unit matrix, 60–62
Online information services, 89, 93. *see also* Information service
Operational planning, 19, 121. *see also* Unit plans; Lesson plans
Organizational information
 database, 17, 94
 file, 35–36, 94
Outputs, *see* Inputs and outputs

P

Passive approach of library media specialist, 10, 89
Perceptions of library media specialist, 11
Planning groups, 32
 district (system level), 34

library media professional support, 34–35
local (building level), 34, 67, 122
Planning information, 63–64
Planning processes, 18–19, 51–68
 comprehensive planning, 18–19, 49, 52–53
 evaluation of plans and processes, 65–68
 five-year plans, 19, 49, 52–54, 65–66
 lesson plans, 121–147
 linear planning, 19–20
 one-year plans, 54–64, 66–67
 operational planning, 20, 121
 planning information database, 63
 planning structures, 52–53
 problem-solving model for, 20–23
 support systems, 23–24, 33–41
 systems approach to, 15–18
 time managment study, 163–166
 top-down planning, 19–20
 unit plans, 121–147
Plans, *see* Five-year plans; Lesson plans; One-year plans; Planning processes; Rolling five-year plans; Unit plans
Priority setting
 in feasibility analysis, 46–47, 50
 for unit plans, 123
Problem-solving feedback perspective, 23
Problem-solving model for planning, 20–23
 acceptance of problem, 21
 analyze components, 22
 brainstorming, 22
 definition of problem, 22
 evaluation, 22
 feedback, 22
 implementation, 22
 selecting the solution, 22
Problem-solving process, *see* Problem-solving model for planning
Processes, *see* Planning processes
Program feasibility analysis, 43, 44–47
 of curriculum support services, 45–47
 of integration of library & information skills instruction and classroom curriculum, 45–47
 priority setting for, 46–47
Program managers, *see* Library & information program managers
Prostano and Prostano, 18, 22

Q

Questions linked to Bloom's cognitive levels, 103

R

Reader's Guide to Periodical Literature, 100, 105
Reading guidance, 11, 90–92, 150–151, 152
  booktalks, 91
  and Big Six Skills, 105
  services checklist, 92
Reading, promotion of, *see* Reading guidance
Reading skills, *see* Reading guidance
Realistic expectations of five-year plans, 53
Reference and information service, *see* Information service
Reflex, 76–77, 78, 81
Regent's Action Plan, 48–49
Reports for curriculum mapping database, 80–82, 84
Research process model, *see* Library research process model
Resource people, 94
Resources, 47, *see also* Resources provision, 47
Resources feasibility analysis, 47–50
  available resources, 47, 49
  cooperation, 50
  priority setting for, 50
  time, professional and support staff, 47–49
Resources provision, 88–90, 152
  services checklist, 90
  sources and systems for location and access skills, 161–162
Review stage of Six-Stage Strategy, 29–30
Role of library media specialist, *see* Library media specialist, role of
Rolling five-year plans, 19, 49, 52–54
  evaluation of, 65–66
  goals and objectives of, 52–53
  introduced, 19
  structure for, 52–53
Rough draft priority list, *see* Priority setting

S

Schedule of curriculum units, 54–57, 124
  elementary school, 55
  secondary school, 56
School librarian, 10. *see also* Library media specialist
School library media center, *see* Library media center
School Library Media Quarterly, 9
School Library media specialist, *see* Library media specialist

Scope and sequence of Big Six Skills curriculum, 104, 106–119
Secondary school
  curriculum map, 82
  lesson plans, 145–147
  schedule of selected subject area units, 56
  skills-by-unit matrix, 59
  support services-by-unit matrix, 62
  unit plans, 139–144
Short-term planning, *see* One-year plans; Operational planning
Six-Stage Strategy, 29–68
  evaluation of, 68
  evaluate plans and processes (Stage Six), 65–68
  review existing situation (Stage One), 29–30
  conduct feasibility analysis (Stage Four), 43–50
  define goals and objectives, (Stage Two), 30–32
  introduced, 6, 24–25, 28
  develop plans (Stage Five), 51–68
  strategy flow, 28
  set up support systems (Stage Three), 33–41
Skills-by-unit matrix, 57–60, 123
  elementary school, 58
  secondary school, 59
Society, information services in, 151–152
Sources and systems for location and access skills, 161–162
Specialization of the library media professional, 160
State curriculum guides, 72
Statement of goals and objectives, 32
Statement of purpose, *see* Mission statement
Strategic planning, *see* One-year plans; Operational planning
Strategy flow (Six-Stage Strategy), 28
Students
  and the Big Six Skills, 106
  and Bloom's taxonomy, 102–104
  higher thinking skills of, 103–104
  and information literacy, 154
  and information problem-solving processes, 150
  use of media and computers, 105
  needs of, 38, 105, 151–152
  and the library research process model, 100–101
Subject area objectives, *see* Curriculum units, subject area objectives of

Subject area units, *see* Curriculum units
Support services, *see* Curriculum support services
Support services-by-unit matrix, 60–62
   elementary school, 61
   secondary school, 62
Support staff, 49
Support systems (Six-Stage Strategy), 23–24, 33–41
   human, 34–35
      district planning group, 34
      library media professional support group, 34–35
      local planning group, 34, 67, 122
   information, 35–41
      curriculum database, 36–37, 63
      curriculum support services checklist, 39–40
      library & information skills curriculum, 37–39
      organizational informational file, 35–36, 94
Synthesis (Big Six Skills), 101, 116–117
System level planning group, *see* District level planning group
Systems approach, 15–18
Systems in education, *see* Education, systems in
Systems model, *see* Input-process-output model
Systems perspective, *see* Systems approach

T
Task definition (Big Six Skills), 101, 108–109
Teachers, 7–8, 48, 62, 67. *see also,* Planning groups
   and curriculum mapping, 76
   and information problem-solving, 159
   and library & information skills instruction, 48
   reading guidance role of, 91
   and unit and lesson plans, 122, 129
Teaching role of library media specialist, 10, 12, 88
Teaching teams, 122, 129
Technological literacy, *see* Computer literacy
Terminal objective (Big Six Skills), 106

Thinking process, *see* Bloom's taxonomy of cognitive objectives
Time demand vs. availability, 48
Time line, *see* Gantt chart
Time management study, 163–166
   data analysis for, 166
   data collection for, 164–165
   planning, 164
   worksheet for, 165
Time, professional and support staff, 47–49
Top-down approach
   to Big Six Skills instruction, 20, 100
   information problem-solving, 38–39, 100
   to library & information skills instruction, 20, 38–39
   to planning, 19–20
   to program feasibility analysis, 46–47
Traditional role of library media specialist, 10
Transferable skills, 103–104, 105. *see also* Big Six Skills curriculum; Bloom's taxonomy of cognitive objectives

U
Unit plans, 121–147
   developing, 122–124
   elementary school, 131–135
   evaluation of, 67
   format for, 124–127
   introduced, 19, 63–64
   priority setting for, 123
   schedule for units, 124
   secondary school, 139–144
   writing, 123–124
The Universal Traveler, 20
U.S. Congress Office of Technology and Assessment, 159
Use of information (Big Six Skills), 101, 114–115

V
Vocabulary, controlled, *see* Controlled vocabulary

W
Wisconsin Department of Public Instruction, Council on Library and Network Development, 14